THE CONVENTIONS OF CRISIS

The Royal Institute of International Affairs is an unofficial body which promotes the scientific study of international questions and does not express opinions of its own. The opinions expressed in this publication are the responsibility of the author.

The Institute gratefully acknowledges the comments and suggestions of the following who read the manuscript on behalf of the Research Committee: Alastair Buchan, Roger Morgan, and Martin Wight.

THE CONVENTIONS OF CRISIS

A Study in Diplomatic Management

Coral Bell

If people do not show wisdom, then in the final analysis
they will come to a clash, like blind moles, and then
reciprocal extermination will begin.

Khrushchev to Kennedy, during the Cuban missile crisis

Published for

THE ROYAL INSTITUTE OF
INTERNATIONAL AFFAIRS

by

OXFORD UNIVERSITY PRESS

LONDON   OXFORD   NEW YORK

1971

Oxford University Press

LONDON   OXFORD   NEW YORK

GLASGOW   TORONTO   MELBOURNE   WELLINGTON

CAPE TOWN   SALISBURY   IBADAN   NAIROBI   DAR ES SALAAM   LUSAKA   ADDIS ABABA

BOMBAY   CALCUTTA   MADRAS   KARACHI   LAHORE   DACCA

KUALA LUMPUR   SINGAPORE   HONG KONG   TOKYO

ISBN 0 19 285054 7

First published as an Oxford University Press paperback
by Oxford University Press, London, 1971

Printed in Great Britain by
The Eastern Press, Limited, London and Reading

CONTENTS

FOREWORD

THIS book began life under the name 'The Incidental Peace', as an essay on the nature of the differences between the diplomatic histories of the interwar and postwar periods. Much of that study survives in the second chapter, but as the focus of my interest moved to the general analysis of crisis and its management I rather reluctantly discarded the original title in favour of the present one, which offers a better clue to the main argument of the work.

My thanks are due to Professor Martin Wight of the University of Sussex, Mr Alastair Buchan, Commandant of the Royal College of Defence Studies, and Dr Roger Morgan of the Royal Institute of International Affairs for kindly reading the manuscript, under its old title, and for many valuable comments. I also want to acknowledge a debt of gratitude to the Australian National University, Canberra, in the shelter of whose generous hospitality most of the book was written, and especially to Professors J. D. B. Miller and Hedley Bull, and Dr T. B. Millar, all of the Institute of Advanced Studies.

C. B.

London
March 1971

1

THE NATURE AND PROVENANCE OF CRISIS

INTERPRETATIONS of the recent past have always a tentative and provisional quality, rope-bridges of hypotheses suspended between rather fragile stanchions of established fact. Yet we cannot avoid asking questions about how we survived yesterday and the day before, if we are to improve our chances for today and tomorrow. This book begins with such a question: how is it that the peace has been preserved since 1945? What are the modes of behaviour which have prevented the endemic crises of the postwar period from turning into central war? (I speak of central war because limited and peripheral wars have been a fairly constant feature of the time.) The answer seems to me to have two parts, one probably over-familiar to those who concern themselves with such things, the other almost unexplored. The over-familiar side has to do with the stabilization of the central balance of power, a project consciously and tenaciously pursued by many hardworking policy-makers since soon after the end of hostilities in 1945. I shall not look further at that aspect of the question in this study,[1] save as it affects the evolution of what I shall call the conventions of crisis management. This evolution was quite unlooked-for, not consciously pursued, almost accidental at least in its earlier days: a by-product of policies devised on other bases. The peace which has been so preserved might therefore be described as incidental, a fringe-benefit, the outcome of serendipity rather than calculation. And that in turn may seem to undermine the whole idea of management, which normally conveys the notion of deliberate manipulation of events or situations in one's own favour.

My argument will be that a process which began in the unwilled fashion I have postulated has been since 1962 much more consciously developed. Conceivably the first man who learned to swim did so because he was caught in floodwaters and found that by striking out at random he had reached the safety of the shore. The technique of the butterfly-stroke, or

[1] There are many books concerned with it, including the author's *Negotiation from Strength: a Study in the Politics of Power* (1962).

the theoretical physics of submerged bodies, are not vitiated by the accidental nature of the original experience.

I shall be preoccupied with conventions rather than rules, laws, theories, or institutions because these more ambitious concepts have not seemed to show to much advantage in the situations that I have examined. Formal institutions like the UN have been only marginally and occasionally useful; many of the more successful modes of management have been strikingly non-legal, even anti-legal in quality; moral considerations have been no more decisive than legal ones, theory has been less apparent than intuition. What has emerged is the growth of conventions—I use this term in the normal sense of a practice based on tacit expectation as to what is ' understood behaviour ', of no special moral or legal sanctity, in a particular society.

The particular society that I have in mind is the society of states, and it might be claimed that what I am calling conventions are in fact just rules of prudence. The distinction between the two is not particularly firm even in domestic societies. No doubt the taboo on eating peas from one's knife is a convention: is it not also a rule of prudence? More seriously, looking at the Highway Code as a spelling-out of the set of expectations current among road-users as a society, one may see in it a whole history of how prudent behaviour hardens into convention, becomes overlaid by moral expectation, and finally may be enforced as law.

I implied earlier that the process of crisis management becomes after 1962 a more conscious enterprise, at least for American policy-makers (who have had until now the major Western role in it). The most conspicuous milestone along this road is a remark of Mr McNamara's, in the aftermath of the Cuban missile crisis, that ' There is no longer any such thing as strategy, only crisis management. ' This rather arguable dictum crystallizes the main anxiety, to my mind, behind the notion: the anxiety that, in situations of crisis, political ends should maintain ascendancy over military means. It was, one might say, Mr McNamara's continuation of an argument that the political members of ' Excom ', the crisis-managing group in October 1962, had had with its military members, the US

Chiefs of Staff, on various points during those thirteen days. From a purely strategic point of view, for instance, there was one desirable line on which to establish the American ships which were to stop the Russian ones bringing missiles to Cuba —a line just beyond the range of MIG aircraft based in Cuba. But from a political point of view, this meant stopping the Russian ships excessively early, giving the decision-makers in Moscow too little time to reflect on the costs of possible alternative modes of reaction. The line finally chosen (at the suggestion of the then British ambassador in Washington) determined that political considerations took precedence over strategic ones: the Russian ships were allowed to continue to a point 500 miles from Cuba. The alleged risk of action by the MIGs never came to anything, and the extra time bought for reflection in Moscow may have been decisive.

One can compare this outcome, for a crisis that did not eventuate in war, with a similar debate between political and strategic considerations during a crisis that did eventuate in war, for instance the 1914 crisis. There were many men in the circle of decision-makers of the Kaiser's Germany who knew that the invasion of Belgium, while militarily convenient, might prove politically disastrous. But in this case, partly because the Schlieffen Plan was so firmly entrenched in the strategic thinking of the High Command, military considerations took precedence over political ones. It would be wrong to imply that this was the only reason why the 1914 crisis produced a war, and the 1962 crisis produced a *détente*. But the image of the 1914 crisis in Kennedy's mind was a factor in his decision-making in the 1962 crisis. The emotional—indeed the moral—impulse behind the search for a theory or a technique of crisis management has been the belief that political considerations *must* maintain ascendancy over military ones in the nuclear age. The case of Vietnam, which will be looked at in due course, represented both a deviation from this view and a misjudgement by the policy-makers of what was at stake, politically and militarily. The result has been a great disaster, moral as well as diplomatic, and a disaster which may well affect America's future role in crisis management. But in many ways this experience of failure may prove more illuminating than other experiences of success.

The academic study of crisis management, at least under that name, dates from shortly after it became a preoccupation of policy-makers. The traditionalist might observe, in rebuttal, that there is an old-fashioned technique called diplomacy, which aims, among other things, at the control of crisis, and a considerable volume of writing about it, which is known as diplomatic history. Undoubtedly crisis management should be considered just a special skill within the general field of diplomacy, as the control of a skid is a special skill within the general field of motoring. But the dynamics of a car in skid are different from those of a car in normal motion, and thus require special study if skidding is to be controlled, or prevented, or even survived. Diplomatic history recounts many crises, but does not generalize about crisis as such. The study of crisis management does attempt this, using as its essential material the histories of actual crises.

That is, it aims to generalize or theorize about crises, rather than to recount the actual events of particular crises. In this it is related to the study which one may call conflict strategy, and it may seem necessary to justify the choice of crisis rather than conflict as the organizing concept of this book. Obviously crises arise out of conflicts, and prima facie it must seem a more thoroughgoing enterprise to investigate the conflicts than merely the crises. I would entirely agree with this proposition, observing only that the investigation of conflict in international politics is so large an enterprise as to be practically coterminous with the study of international politics in general. There are very few relationships between states which do not contain elements of conflict. Crisis is a smaller, more manageable, more clearly defined, more *isolable* phenomenon than conflict, and therefore the concept of crisis has seemed more useful for the particular study that I have in mind.

The late emergence of crisis or conflict as central preoccupations of students of international politics is perhaps an indication of a too-persistent optimism among academics in the subject generally. After the First World War, when the study of international relations began filtering into the universities, war and crisis tended to be thought of as temporary and irrational hangovers from a less enlightened period of history, the product of warrior castes like the Prussian *Junkers* or of outmoded varieties of economic organization. The new Jerusalem of peace and harmony among the nations seemed just around the corner, whether one believed the way to it lay through Lenin's prescription of international socialism, or Woodrow Wilson's of collective security, or that of some bright young professor of international relations for ensuring the rule of international law. Fifty years on, the world has lived with the experience of seeing the two great states which each claim to be Lenin's true interpreter close to war with each other; two organizations which each have represented attempts at the principle of collective security—the League and the UN—have proved only marginally effective; and international law has proved irrelevant to the control of the conflicts which threaten peace. War as an institution flourishes as robustly as ever it did: there have been about eighty sets of armed encounters[2] of an indentifiable sort in what is usually called the postwar period.

The new Jerusalem of peace and harmony among the nations seems a lot further off than it did fifty years ago, round many more difficult corners. Moreover, some lines of research in ethology seem to suggest that the sources of conflict among human groups run as deep as the instincts that ensured the survival of particular species in a pre-human evolutionary phase, and that the social cohesion of groups like nations may depend largely on the existence of an external enemy: a licensed target for the discharge of hostility that would other-wise disrupt the society itself.[3] Whether or not one accepts the analogies between animal and human behaviour (and they sometimes seem startlingly close) it is clear that group behaviour often falls into patterns rather of instinctual or tribal reaction than of rational calculation. Such patterns are not readily re-shaped by arrangements that belong to the superstructure of life—organizations or law or even changes in the formalities of economic relationship. Thus conflict between human

---

[2] Listed in David Wood, *Conflict in the Twentieth Century* (1968). Each of his categories of armed conflict shows a growth in the postwar period—or more properly the period since 1945.

[3] See Konrad Lorenz, *On Aggression* (1966).

groups (nations or other entities) is not readily going to be organized or reasoned or resolved out of existence. The propensity to conflict must be accepted as a continuing fact of human life, even though, among nations, the technical means for pursuing conflicts are now so monstrously efficient as to threaten the end of human life itself.

This may seem a defeatist starting point for the study of crisis management but it is in fact the only hopeful one. A sense of the permanence of conflict, and the probability of crisis, between nations is the only adequate incentive to serious work on managing crises and limiting the destructiveness of the armed hostilities they may evoke.

It is part of the business of academic analysis to reflect on the behaviour of policy-makers: to try to discern, on the evidence available, the factors which apparently make for success and those which apparently make for disaster. The proof of the pudding is in the eating, as the saying goes. And there is no other proof. That is, the results of a piece of crisis management can only be observed in history, not established by theory. That does not mean that no theory is possible: only that theory is the stepchild of the activity, rather than its parent.[4]

We have now to ask what is the nature of crisis, and what its provenance: that is, from what sources it may be shown to come. The word is much over-used, probably because it is so handy for newspaper headlines and carries a built-in promise of drama. But most of the usages—industrial crisis, economic crisis, marital crisis, student crisis, football crisis—are legitimate enough because ' crisis ', as far as its Greek derivation goes, only means a decision point, or the turning point of an illness, and almost all relationships, whether between man and wife, parent and child, employer and employee, or political groups do have turning points, or decision points. There are some

[4] Many writers concerned with crisis or conflict would take a more optimistic view than this about the sources from which theories and generalizations might be derived, holding that model-building techniques of various sorts are, or will be, important founts of theory about the real world of international politics. The author does not share this view, and would maintain that techniques like game theory, content analysis, operational research, systems analysis, and simulation have already been in use for long enough to have demonstrated their limitations as well as their occasional (and marginal) usefulness.

characteristic kinds of crisis behaviour or crisis techniques which are common to crises of various sorts. Even the vocabulary is applicable to many fields: deterrence and ultimata, bargaining and compromise, signalling and intermediaries, all transfer without essential change from one kind of relationship to another. However, this study will be concerned with international crises, and will consider other sorts only for passing illustration. That is, it will be concerned with the turning points or decision points in relations between states.

International crises are of two main sorts, which I propose to call adversary and intramural. Adversary crises are, obviously, between powers regarding themselves as adversaries. Intramural crises are crises within the walls of an alliance, or the power sphere of one of the dominant powers, or a regional organization.

I shall be preoccupied mostly with crises affecting the powers of the central nuclear balance, because the policy choices of their decision-makers have consequences of such gravity. The crises of local balances and of regional organizations are often of great interest, but they do not usually carry such a freight of potential danger to the rest of the world. The military consequences of such crises, if any, mostly remain local, unless the dominant powers become involved.

I shall use the term ' dominant powers ' to mean just that, i.e. the powers which move and shake the world, dominate international politics, at any particular time. In the contemporary world these powers are only three—America, Russia, and China. I do not use the traditional term ' great powers ' because there are some states, for instance Japan, to which it seems churlish to deny that description, but which do not yet play the role in international politics characteristic of the other three.

Note that the category is not that of ' world powers ', i.e. powers able to make themselves militarily effective everywhere, nor yet ' super-powers ', a term invented in the immediate postwar period to distinguish the USA and the USSR as powers whose military and other potential then seemed to put them in a totally distinct category from the rest. The category of super-power was more relevant for the twelve years or so after 1945 than it is now or is likely to be in future. The category of dominant power is also intended to facilitate comparison of the crisis behaviour of the dominant powers of the postwar period with those of the interwar period and earlier diplomatic history. In the interwar period the powers which dominated world politics were seven: Germany, Britain, France, America, Russia, Japan, and Italy. In the 1911–14 period the group of dominant powers should probably be counted as five. I mention these figures because the number of sets of decision-makers having a major influence on events appears germane to the level of control and predictability in crisis diplomacy.[5]

Local balances and regional alliance systems also have both varieties of crisis, so that altogether there are four distinguishable categories:

1. Adversary crises of the central balance (like Cuba, or Munich).

2. Intramural crises of the power spheres or alliances systems of the dominant powers (Cyprus as an intramural crisis of the NATO alliance, or Czechoslovakia as an intramural crisis of the Soviet power sphere).

3. Adversary crises of local balances (Kashmir 1965 as a crisis of the Indo-Pakistan balance; May–June 1967 as a crisis of the Israeli-Arab balance).

4. Intramural crises of regional alliances or organizations (Biafra as an intramural crisis of the OAU).

These distinctions are not purely academic: I shall suggest later that one of the more successful techniques of management of adversary crisis has been to turn it into intramural crisis, so an understanding of these two categories is necessary for the analysis. Likewise it is essential to distinguish between the management role of the dominant powers in crises of the central balance, and their power to intervene in or manipulate crises of local balances (as for instance Soviet manipulation of the early stages of the 1967 Middle East crisis).

[5] The number of dominant powers in the society of states has fluctuated only between two and about ten over the past two centuries. There are some interesting studies of the relation between numbers and stability in the system in, for instance, the writings of Kenneth Waltz, Morton Kaplan, Stanley Hoffman, and Richard Rosecrance. See especially Waltz, ‘ The Stability of a Bipolar World ’, *Daedalus* (Cambridge, Mass.), spring 1964, pp. 881–909.

Most of the true international crises of the postwar period fit into one of the four categories suggested. But I have had to invent two other categories, pseudocrisis and subcrisis, for episodes which are usually called crises but which do not, on examination, quite live up to the name. For instance, I regard the Tongking Gulf ' crisis ' of 1964 as actually a pseudocrisis, a sort of public relations exercise for a decision taken on another basis than the apparent one.[6] The U-2 ' crisis ' of 1960 was actually a subcrisis (adversary); the MLF a subcrisis (intramural).

The reason for these categories will emerge as we examine the nature of the true crisis. What is the process which produces the ' turning point ' or ' decision point ' which is its central quality? To my mind the essence of true crisis in any given relationship is that the conflicts within it rise to a level which threatens to transform the nature of the relationship. In adversary crisis, the potential transformation is from peace to war; in intramural crisis it is from alliance to rupture. Though I devised this definition with international crises in mind, I think it is applicable to most relationships in which crisis may be expected. The concept is of normal strain rising to the level of breaking strain. Thus a true crisis between man and wife might threaten to transform the relationship from marriage to divorce; between employer and employee it might threaten the change from work contract to firing or strike. This notion of a breaking strain provides the necessary theoretical criterion of distinction between subcritical stresses (often loosely called crises) and true crises, even though at the policy level it is not always easy to apply since the breaking strain of a diplomatic relationship is not so readily established as that of a length of rope. The decision whether a particular diplomatic episode ought to be assigned to the category of true crisis, or that of subcrisis, must be a tentative judgement based on the evidence available. I classify the U-2 incident as a subcrisis, since the present evidence is that, though it certainly worsened relations between the United States and the Soviet Union, the stresses remained subcritical: there was never any risk of war.

[6] The Pentagon papers, insofar as they had been published when this book was in proof, appeared amply to substantiate this judgement.

The category of pseudocrisis may be more difficult to justify. It is rather like that of psychosomatic illness: the apparent cause may not be the true cause, yet the symptoms are as indicative of trouble as those which stem from organic causes. The incident in the Bay of Tongking in August 1964 was of a very minor sort: a couple of North Vietnamese torpedo boats made a pass which was not only well provoked but quite ineffective at two American destroyers supporting South Vietnamese action against the North Vietnamese coast. In terms of its own significance this incident could hardly be judged to meet my criterion of seriously raising the level of conflict within the relationship concerned, that between the United States and North Vietnam. Prima facie, the only relationship in which it was genuinely significant was that between President Johnson and the US Senate, since Senator Fulbright was induced by this episode to introduce the Tongking Gulf resolution. That is why I described it as a public relations exercise. Yet this pseudo-crisis, if the category be allowed, was also a signal of a real crisis in the land battle in South Vietnam, just as the psycho-somatic illness is a signal of real trouble.

Finally, one might mention a category of domestic political crisis which may be either a result or a cause of international crisis. The Suez crisis precipitated a domestic political crisis in Britain, though not in France or Israel. Contrariwise, the international crisis over Czechoslovakia (either 1938 or 1968) was precipitated by an earlier domestic political crisis in that country. I shall consider domestic crisis only when it is inter-twined with international crisis.

Many episodes of diplomatic history, such as the Suez adventure, are complex enough to seem assignable to the category either of intramural crisis or of adversary crisis. In such cases I propose to classify them according to which set of dangers appears to have been the most real and important. Thus I would class Suez primarily as an intramural crisis, because the dangers to the functioning of the Western alliance were greater than the dangers to the general peace. (In fact the dangers to the general peace were slight or negligible.) On the other hand, Cuba was clearly an adversary crisis, though with intramural aspects (an impact on the Western alliance

which was real, though slight in comparison either with the
impact on the Sino-Soviet alliance or with the risks to the
general peace). Most major crises have had both adversary and
intramural aspects, but it is not usually difficult to assign them
to the one category or the other on the basis of where the predominant dangers lay. The conflict between the Soviet Union
and China is particularly interesting in this respect, because it
illustrates the gradation from one variety of crisis to the other.
The early crises of this conflict, up to 1962, were intramural, in
that the Sino-Soviet alliance was still more or less functioning.
The later crises have certainly been adversary.[7]

What are the criteria for success in crisis management?
Here we must again emphasize the distinction between adversary crisis (crisis between powers defining themselves as potential military adversaries) and intramural crisis (crisis between
states within a particular alliance system or acknowledged
sphere of influence or regional organization). It is, naturally,
adversary crises that most people are concerned about, since
these are the ones which carry most risk of war. In fact, an
adversary crisis is usually recognized by a sudden sharp rise in
the apprehension of war. One might therefore be tempted to
say that the avoidance of war is the only criterion for success
in the management of adversary crisis. But this single criterion
is not adequate, because it would oblige us to classify as a
success, for instance, the management of the Munich crisis of
1938. War was certainly avoided on that occasion, but only to
be incurred a year later, on worse terms. Nor can this be
rationalized as a postponement strategically justified: the

[7] Some other writers in this field have used rather different concepts of crisis
from those I am using. Alastair Buchan, for instance, writes: ' A crisis normally
implies a deliberate challenge and a deliberated response, of a kind which both
sides hope will change the course of history in their favour. . . . The crisis period
covers the formulation of the challenge, the definition of the issue, the decision on
the appropriate reaction to the challenge, the impact of such a reaction upon the
adversary, and the clarification of his response.' (*Crisis Management* (1964), p. 21.)
Oran Young defines crisis as ' a set of *rapidly* unfolding events which raises the
impact of destabilizing forces in the general international system or any of its
subsystems substantially above " normal " (i.e. average) levels and *increases the
likelihood of violence* occurring in the system. ' (*The Intermediaries* (1967), p. 10; my
italics.) Both these definitions are admirably clear and lucid, but both of them
would narrow the category of crisis to a smaller assortment of episodes than I
have been concerned with.

' time bought ' by Munich was most successfully used by Hitler. The war incurred in 1939 was probably fought on worse terms, lasted longer, and was more disastrous in its effects than the war which might have been incurred in 1938. If Munich was a successful piece of crisis management, the success was Hitler's.[8]

Since there are always at least two sets of actual or aspirant crisis managers in any international crisis, one may assess the degree of success or failure from the standpoint of either of them. But one can also use criteria for success derived from the interests, as one sees them, of the society of states as a whole, and by most judgements this would involve consideration of whether the settlement forwarded the interests of justice, or stability, or both. Bearing this in mind, the criteria that I suggest for judging success in adversary crisis management are three:

1.   Has the probability of war between the chief adversaries been increased or diminished, or has any mitigation been made to the conflict between them?

2.   What has been the effect on the power position of either over the short and longer terms?

3.   Has any contribution been made to the conventions and techniques of crisis management?

If we apply these criteria to the most fully documented of all recent crises, the Cuban missile crisis of 1962, we see that the crisis was a clear success by the first and third criteria: the prospect of war between America and Russia clearly has been much less since the crisis than it was before. And the techniques and conventions evolved during the crisis have clearly contributed to the management of other, later, crises: the 'hot line ' for instance, was used by both the Americans and Russians during the 1967 Middle Eastern crisis. As to the second criterion, the results of the crisis were rather more mixed and ambiguous: certainly over the short term it enhanced the power position of the United States in the world generally and in the Latin American area in particular. But this effect perhaps

---

[8] This is a point still debated with some passion, especially by those who were involved in the Munich settlement. Perhaps the strongest case to be made in rebuttal of the view I have conveyed here is the one which turns on the absolute necessity of time to build British air defences, no matter what other elements in the power balance were adversely affected by the year between Munich and Danzig.

did not long outlive President Kennedy himself. Taking into account the development of Soviet naval and missile capacity, which seems to have been at least partially inspired or hastened by the crisis, one might have to say that over the longer term it was the Soviet power position which showed most improvement.

The Cuban missile crisis is well documented, chiefly because so many of the people who surrounded Kennedy were articulate intellectuals. In the case of most other crises it is more difficult to reach a firm judgement of whether the crisis management can be called successful, and if so, for which set of crisis managers.

As to intramural crises (crises within the walls of an alliance system or a power sphere) one may again make the judgement of relative success on the basis of three different criteria. First, is the ability of the alliance to function impaired or maintained? Secondly, what is the influence of the crisis settlement on the degree of satisfaction of the members with their positions within it? And thirdly (since the dominant power of the alliance or power sphere is almost always involved), what is the impact of the settlement on the credibility or ' credit ' of this power? From the point of view of the dominant member, the alliance or power sphere is an instrument for its own security, so that its continued functioning as such is the primary factor in considering the management of an intramural crisis. But each member of the alliance assesses it as a system of costs and benefits, and their individual assessments may be modified by any particular episode of crisis management. Thus when considering, for instance, the Czech crisis of 1968–9 as an intramural crisis of the Warsaw Pact, and considering the Russian management of this crisis from the spring of 1968 to the summer of 1969, one might be obliged to put it down as a success from the point of view of maintaining Eastern Europe as a buffer zone for Russian security, but a failure on the other criteria mentioned. Some episodes of intramural crisis for the NATO alliance system, such as, for instance, the Suez crisis of 1956, might return similar mixed verdicts.

In any given crisis, I shall refer to the power which seeks to make changes as the revisionist, and the power which seeks to prevent such change as the *status quo* power. There are various other pairs of terms which might do, such as ' challenger ' and ' defender ', but they seem to carry an excessive freight of value judgements. Neither the proposal to change things, nor the determination to resist change is necessarily good in itself. What one has to judge in each case is whether the proposed change will advance or damage the ability of the people affected to pursue the good life. Making such a judgement is hardly ever easy, and often very difficult indeed.

There is a further problem in this usage in that, to my mind, powers should be placed in the category of revisionist or *status quo*, with respect to any particular situation, not in terms of what they *want* (since wants are illimitable) but in terms of *what they will take risks to get or keep*. Using this criterion it becomes obvious that revisionism in our sense is often more ostensible or declaratory than real, and this is helpful in the understanding of some episodes of, especially, Russian crisis management.

Finally, I shall suggest a category which I call the crisis slide. There are periods in history when individual crises remain distinct, like isolated boulders rolling down a mountainside. Each may do some damage, and present some dangers, but they are events discrete in themselves, like the Chanak or the Corfu crises of the early twenties. There are other periods when the boulders, or the crises, not only come thick and fast, but seem, as it were, to repercuss off each other until the whole mountainside, or the whole society of states, begins to crumble. These episodes are what I mean by crisis slides, and I would argue that there was one in the period 1936–9, and an earlier one in the period 1906–14. Even an isolated crisis might start a major war, obviously, but it seems more likely for war to eventuate from a crisis slide. The foundations of peace are stronger than many people suppose, and are not very apt to be knocked out by one episode. Fortunately there has been no real crisis slide in the postwar period, as yet, though possibly the events of 1948–50 came close to being one. It must clearly be a major point in the management of individual crises that they be prevented from gathering the momentum that will allow them to turn themselves into a crisis slide. To my mind, the essential characteristic of the crisis slide is that *the decision-makers of one or more of the dominant powers believe that they see the options available to them steadily closing down to the single option of war or unlimited defeat.* I shall argue later for this interpretation of the events of 1936–9, and of 1906–14, and shall hazard an explanation of why such a disaster has so far been avoided since 1945.

As to the provenance of crisis, the sources from which it can be shown to come, the short answer is that it may arise from any conflict of will or interest between states, whether they define each other as adversaries or allies. The provenance of particular kinds of crisis will be examined later. In many ways the dynamics of crisis appear much the same, independent of the particular conflicts from which they stem. The great and often destructive river of international politics is fed from many sources, and its cross-currents, the conflicts between states, provide various levels of hazard. Yet the rapids and whirlpools —the crises—establish their own laws, and the business of negotiating them is quite separate from the business of charting the currents.

TWO PERIODS OF CRISIS: SOME COMPARISONS

THE two periods of diplomatic history which seem to offer the most useful comparisons in crisis management, for my purposes, are the twenty-one years from 1918 to 1939, and the twenty-five years of the postwar period to date. The period from 1815 to 1906 might seem to offer more examples of success, but it is necessary to be chary of analogies with crises stemming from quite different systems of communications, and from decision-makers selected by largely different political processes. These are the essential factors of change: the nature of the decision-makers, the communication between them, and the means available to them to make their decisions effective. These factors are not widely different (save in one respect) as between the interwar and postwar periods: they are less alike, but still rather alike as between these periods and the prelude to the First World War, and they become increasingly different as one retreats back towards 1815, especially beyond the watershed marked by the general use of telegraphy, from the 1850s. Such considerations do not entirely vitiate the usefulness of comparisons with the nineteenth-century system, and I shall use some in due course, but without placing much weight on them as a source of generalization.

The most obvious difference, in terms of diplomatic history, between the interwar period and the postwar period is that, if I may use my categories, the interwar system fell into the condition that I call crisis slide towards general war only eighteen years after the end of World War I, in 1936, whereas in the twenty-five years since World War II the decision-makers of the dominant powers have managed to avoid any such catastrophe. The essence of a crisis slide, as I have indicated, is not merely that crises come thick and fast, and from several angles, and that the crisis management increases the probability of war between the main adversaries, but that the process of events backs one or more of the states concerned into a corner from which its decision-makers see no way out except war. One may readily see this effect in the case of British decision-makers in the 1936–9 crisis slide. The remilitarization of the Rhineland in March 1936 ended the option of believing that the Versailles settlement could be maintained; the development of the Axis between Germany and Italy ended the hope that a balance of power coalition could be created within Europe to restrain Hitler; the ease of the *Anschluss* in 1938 made it clear how vulnerably eastern Europe lay open to Hitler; the Munich Agreement was the last quaver of the hope that if the Germans were conceded what they might be deemed entitled to (the annexation of the German-speaking folk of the Sudetenland to the Reich) they would not demand more; Prague showed the vanity of this hope and precipitated the guarantees to Rumania and Poland which were intended to restrain Germany by making an unambiguous commitment. When this last hope failed (and incidentally succeeded in depriving Britain of all room for manoeuvre *vis-à-vis* Russia) there was no option in September 1939 but the British declaration of war.

The concatenation of events from the Moroccan crisis of 1906 or the Bosnian crisis of 1908–9 to August 1914 perhaps represents an equivalent crisis slide. Several of the dominant powers had come to assume that the options available to them had narrowed down to war or unlimited defeat. Austria-Hungary felt the pressure of demands of the nationalists as an intolerable threat to its imperial life: that it would ' lose its position as a great power if it stood any more nonsense from Serbia '; Germany had contracted in 1909 to support Austria if Russia intervened on behalf of Serbia; France saw a victory for the Germanic powers as catastrophic to its own security; Britain had committed itself to the *entente* with France and the security of Belgium, and felt as well the rising threat of German ambitions at sea. The assassination of the Archduke was the boulder that set off this avalanche, rolling down on the remnants of the old order.[1]

To establish the reasons why such a crisis slide has not yet eventuated in the postwar period, we must look at the way in

[1] One might date this crisis slide from 1908 or 1911 (Agadir) rather than 1906, but I think there is a case for preferring the longer period, the sullen exasperation of Austria being one decisive factor. See F. R. Bridge, ' The Diplomatic Relations between Great Britain and Austria-Hungary, 1898–1903 ' (unpublished Ph.D. thesis of the University of London, 1966) for a study of this period.

which the decision-makers of the dominant powers make their choices during crises. There is one overwhelming factor of difference as against the two earlier periods, consciousness of which must suffuse all discussion of the later period: the existence of nuclear weapons. Certainly the new weapons have enormously increased the potential penalties of error in crisis management. Decision-makers in the earlier periods were like drivers conducting powerful and ill-steering trucks along badly made roads in conditions of poor visibility, and under the urge of a certain competitiveness on the part of the owners. They still are, only now some of the trucks are known to be loaded with nitroglycerine. This knowledge powerfully reinforces caution, no doubt. But it would be wrong to assume that inter-war decision-makers took a lighthearted view of the penalties of allowing crises to deteriorate into war. Quite the contrary was the case, at least as far as Western politicians and others in the 1930s were concerned. (I do not speak here of the pre-1914 period.) Their expectations were surprisingly similar to those generally entertained at present about the onset of nuclear war: immediate, severe, almost irreparable devastation through air strike. Writing in 1923, a sober historian like Webster could say that the world now knew that another war would mean the complete overthrow of civilization.[2] People were expected to break emotionally under the strain of twentieth-century war much more readily than they actually did: a great many psychiatric beds were provided, for instance, in England in 1939. In fact, from various indices such as the suicide rate, one might say that the percentage of alienation and emotional disorientation apparently *decreases* under war conditions, the greater human solidarity induced by the sense of being part of a community under attack presumably offsetting the dangers and discomforts suffered. Even when these reach an extreme level, as in Berlin during the final months of continuous bombing and shelling, civilian morale proved a good deal tougher than expected. It was only in the very last weeks, with surrender and occupation known to be imminent, that morale collapsed.

There is, however, one very important respect in which the

[2] In an essay, ' The Congress of Vienna 1814–15 and the Conference of Paris 1919 ', reprinted in W. N. Medlicott, ed., *From Metternich to Hitler* (1963), p. 13.

weight on crisis decision-makers of their expectations about the
nature of the war which their decisions may incur has changed.
This weight has been more *symmetrically* distributed in the postwar than in the interwar period. That is, decision-makers on
both sides of the hill seem to have had about an equal sense of
the penalties of war. If anything the chief putative revisionist
power for most of the period, the USSR, has had the more
powerful and emotionally loaded memory of what these penalties have been. This ought also to have been true of the chief
interwar revisionist power, Germany, but for complicated
reasons it was not. Hitler's pathological personal determination
to reverse the verdict of 1918, the Nazi metaphysic of the
virtues of race, violence, and self-sacrifice for the ideological
cause, the self-assurance generated by a string of easy national
successes, Goering's assurances (and perhaps belief) that he
could protect the populace from air strike—all these factors
certainly tended to the effect that both the decision-makers and
the underlying population were less preoccupied with the
penalties of war than was the case for the other states concerned.
In the postwar situation, all the statesmen involved have mani-
fested a sort of intensified version of the Western politicians'
anxieties in the 1938–9 period. Some analysts would maintain
that this is not true in the case of Chinese leaders, and it certainly
is possible to quote flights of Maoist oratory which tend to
indicate an excessively sanguine view of the results and aftermath of nuclear war. The Russians frequently do quote this
rhetoric as part of their case against China. The contrast between it and Chinese operational policy in actual crisis situations will be considered later.

There is, however, a more impersonal factor of difference
than this, and one which may be seen in the names that the
usage of journalists or historians has attached to the two
epochs: the ' twenty years' crisis ' and ' the cold war '. The
' twenty years' crisis ' was E. H. Carr's term, and his use of the
word crisis is somewhat less specific than that which I have
adopted. Actually within that twenty-year span there were
long periods of *détente*, and only the final three or at most four
years can reasonably be regarded as a crisis slide. But Carr's
term reflects the way a powerful analytic imagination saw a

just-completed patch of history in 1939.[3] It was a retrospective verdict on a historical process only defined by its end. The cold war, on the other hand, was so named almost before it had been declared: by Walter Lippmann in a pamphlet written in 1947.[4] The moment which is usually taken as the declaration of the cold war is March 1947, the Truman Doctrine, though one might equally date it from March 1946, from Churchill's 'iron curtain' speech at Fulton, Missouri. Truman was present at this speech, and was undoubtedly much influenced by Churchill's formulation of the emerging shape of world politics. But whether one takes the moment when it is first signalled (Churchill's speech) or the moment when it is made formal and official (Truman's message to Congress), the import is much the same: the acceptance and declaration of an adversary relationship.

I would argue that this *early* recognition of an adversary relationship is the most important single political difference between the postwar and interwar periods, roughly on the grounds that to concede the existence of a conflict is the essential first step to managing the crises to which it gives rise. However, I would also argue that this recognition, in its initial stages, was substantially based on misapprehension. The policy-maker chiefly concerned was somewhat in the situation of the man in Lewis Carroll's verse:

> He thought he saw a Theorem
> That questioned him in Greek
> He looked again and saw it was
> The Middle of Next Week . . .

That is to say, the genesis of the Truman Doctrine involved a Western interpretation of Soviet capabilities and intentions at the time which is now impossible to sustain. The over-dramatic reporting of the US ambassador in Athens of the threat represented by the guerrillas in the north, combined with Truman's amateur-strategist view of the vital importance of Turkey and the Straits, plus the temporarily acute prostration of Europe, including Britain, by the particularly bad winter of

---

[3] *The Twenty Years' Crisis, 1919–1939* was completed in the summer of 1939, and the first edition was published just after the outbreak of the war.
[4] *The Cold War: a Study in US Foreign Policy* (1947).

1946–7, created conditions in which the always lively mind of the pivotal decision-maker involved, Dean Acheson, the US Under-Secretary of State, developed a rather excessive conviction of the imminence of a take-over bid by Russia for Western Europe. Acheson wrote at the time:

There was small likelihood that the governmental, political, and economic institutions of Western Europe could survive the end of hope and the drastic deprivation of elemental necessities which would follow the exhaustion of ability to purchase abroad. The overwhelming probability was that control—except in England— would pass to those who had the daring and organization, with foreign backing, to take over dictatorial power and who could claim special standing as advocates with the power which controlled all the resources from Poland to the maritime provinces of the Pacific. It was this situation, rather than any intrinsic appeal of the doctrines of communism, even stimulated by skillful and well organized and endowed propaganda, which may have led the policy-makers in the Kremlin to think that they were about to win the greatest prize of history without military effort on their part—a power system extending from the Atlantic to the Pacific including the Mediterranean and North Africa and most of the population and resources of the world.[5]

The evidence that the policy-makers in the Kremlin entertained any such optimistic notions of the chances of Communism in Western Europe now seems rather thin. Stalin was a sober, cautious man, generally sceptical of any power advantages for Russia which did not rest firmly on the bayonets of the Red Army. Even with regard to China, where victory for the Communists was in fact only two years away at this point, he had been quite recently insisting to Mao that the bourgeoisie in China was still very strong. He was intent on consolidating, by political repression and military occupation, the buffer zone in Eastern Europe which the wartime movement of the armies had won for the USSR (and other Russian decision-makers have remained willing to use all necessary modes of military and political oppression to this end ever since). But he was by no means an adventurist in the sense of one willing to take serious risks to press a contested and doubtful advantage. This was

[5] Introduction to *The United States in World Affairs, 1947–1948* (1948).

already visible in his handling of the Iranian crisis of 1946 (over the retention of Russian forces in Iranian Azerbaijan beyond the date due for their departure). The Russian government was quite prepared to use the vague threats to Iran's integrity implied by the presence of these troops (with the clear ' signals ' of a possible ' autonomous ' Azerbaijan) to exact an oil concession from the Iranian government. But once it had become clear that the US government was seriously concerning itself with the matter (a fact assiduously signalled in a series of speeches by the US ambassador in Teheran), and the Red Army was actually out of Iran, the Russians acquiesced quite blandly in the Iranians' denunciation of the oil concession, and their re-imposition of control by force in Azerbaijan. One has to say that in this early encounter in the definition of attitudes by the two new dominant powers, the Russian crisis management was distinctly cautious and tentative, more so perhaps than the American.[6]

But in making these judgements one is exercising what Charles Bohlen, one of the State Department men involved, has called ' twenty-twenty hindsight '. The 1947 view which now seems so alarmist was not exclusive to Acheson, or to right-wing persons. The reporting from Moscow to the State Department of such a (later) well-known dove as George Kennan, and of Averell Harriman, tended to the same picture of the Soviet Union as a power bent on extending rather than consolidating its sphere of influence, either by military or political means, or by some mixture of the two. The expansive revolutionary effervescence of Yugoslavia (still at this point a Soviet ally), the Soviet verbal intransigence against Turkey, the guerrilla campaign in Greece, the doctrines associated with Zhdanov, the Soviet ostensible revolutionary tradition, and so on, all helped confirm the picture of a state which not only was determined to expand the area of ' the revolution ', or its own power sphere (the two being regarded at this time as coterminous) but was to some extent obliged to do so by its own ideological principles. But at this point my distinction between what a country *wants*, and what it will take serious risks *to get* must be

[6] The diplomatic finesse of the then Iranian Prime Minister, Ghavam es-Sultaneh, was also a major factor in the management of this crisis.

remembered. In terms of its declaratory policy the USSR has been since the Revolution a revisionist power in the diplomatic sense, looking to a total transformation of the society of states. But it is difficult to think of many episodes over the half-century in which it has actually taken risks to promote the fortunes of the revolution, or of revolutionary powers. Cuba would be the one exception. The USSR has in operational policy defined itself as a *status quo* power, by being much more willing to take risks to keep assets acquired (such as the buffer zone in Eastern Europe) than to acquire new ones. (There is nothing unique to the Russians about this: it is one of the psychological assets of the *status quo* power in crisis situations that people on the whole are more ready to take risks to keep what they have than to get something more.) But the USSR, or Russia before it, in each of the periods we are considering has tended to waver ambiguously between a *status quo* and a revisionist stance. Since 1917 the ambiguity has arisen from the combination of a declaratory policy which is revisionist, with an operational policy which is largely *status quo*.

To repeat, taking the 1947 situation as a whole one may argue that the Truman Doctrine was founded on a view of Russian policy which did not in fact have much base in reality, though it seemed reasonable enough given the evidence available at the time. And the Truman Doctrine was, as its critics said, a declaration of war: the cold war. Or, to put it more analytically, the Truman Doctrine is what marks the conscious acceptance by the United States of an adversary relationship with the USSR, and, slightly less consciously, American acceptance of the role of leader of the *status quo* coalition in this encounter. The *status quo* coalition for Europe was formalized into NATO two years later, and has persisted, a little tattered but basically unchanged, for more than twenty years.

The cold war has had a bad press, and one feels somewhat of a devil's advocate in putting forward arguments tending to show its usefulness as part of a historic process. But one may, I think, describe it as, among other things, a learning curve in crisis management. In any new, complex enterprise, like producing advanced weapons systems, or nuclear power stations, or journeying into space, a learning curve may be discerned: that is, the enterprise is conducted with more confidence, more skill, a reduced tendency to overlook vital considerations, as experience is gained. The disasters and near-misses of the early period are part of the cost of the successes of the later period. Similarly in crisis management, a success in the later years of the cold war, like Cuba 1962, is in part accounted for by the learning curve of the cold war itself. Of course even experienced managers on a late sector of a learning curve may deviate into almost inexplicable error: consider the production of the Edsel at a point when the Ford company was indisputably far advanced on its institutionalized learning curve. (Or for that matter the RB-211 contract at a point when the same was true for Rolls-Royce.) But crisis management is certainly learned behaviour, and one must therefore expect the benefits of the learning curve to show up sooner or later. The replacement of one set of individual decision-makers by a different set, as after an American presidential election, complicates the shape of the curve, and one might have to expect some downturn for each new set of decision-makers. Nevertheless, the learning process is largely institutionalized in a government, as in a company. There is a real sense in which the gains of Kennedy's time were incorporated into Nixon's policy.

If it is accepted that the recognition of an adversary relationship, and an unambiguous definition of the leadership of the *status quo* coalition were established very early in the postwar period, it becomes of interest to ask why these attitudes were hardly established at all in the interwar period, until the (literally) bitter end. Re-reading Carr's accounts of the earlier period,[7] one can see a number of factors which explain the difference. One of them is visible in Carr's own writings: Western left-liberal guilt feelings towards Germany. Germany was, so to speak, defined as a victim, not an adversary, from the earliest reassessments of Versailles, in the Weimar period, and this definition-as-a-victim persisted right up until after the Munich settlement. Its last remnants were kicked aside during the march into Prague. Mr A. J. P. Taylor once irritated a

[7] Both in *The Twenty Years' Crisis, 1919–1939* (1939) and *International Relations between the two World Wars, 1919–1939* (1947).

great many people by writing that Munich was a victory for all that was best in British life,[8] but this is a reasonable interpretation enough: appeasement as a mode of crisis management was based on the sense that an injustice ought to be remedied, even after twenty years, and the faith (fatuous in this case) that remedying it would produce reconciliation. As often happens in international politics, a moral impulse had disastrous consequences, but one cannot for that reason deny the moral feeling behind Chamberlain's belief that the Germans had real grievances which should be removed by appeasement.

As far as the recognition of an adversary relationship with Russia was concerned, there were no such guilt feelings among the particular decision-makers involved to inhibit its growth after 1945. Rather the contrary in fact: the Western leadership came out of the Grand Alliance not only with a great many resentments against Stalin's conduct of politics and hostilities in the later years of the war, but also the conviction (not altogether unreasonable) that the Nazi-Soviet pact had given Hitler the green light for launching the attack on Poland, and that Stalin was therefore almost equally the author of the world's catastrophe. These attitudes among policy-makers were of course not made public until the Fulton speech: hence the degree of shock occasioned by it.

There is one equivalent in the postwar period to the Germany-as-victim viewpoint in the interwar period. As I said, the cold war has had a bad press, and though this can mostly be put down to a reasonable (though to my mind mistaken) view of it as a *prelude to* hostilities rather than a *substitute for* hostilities, it does show some slight influence, as in the interwar German case, of a guilt-ridden liberal determination to define the adversary as a victim. The clearest instances of this influence are the interpretations which date the cold war's origin from 1917 or 1918 (the interventions in Russia)[9] and represent it as essentially a Western effort to destroy the Communist revolu-

[8] *The Origins of the Second World War* (1961), p. 189: ' It was a triumph for all that was best and most enlightened in British life; a triumph for those who had preached equal justice between peoples; a triumph for those who had courageously denounced the harshness of Versailles.'

[9] See, for instance, D. F. Fleming's *The Cold War and its Origins, 1917–1960*, vol. 1, *1917–1950* (1961).

tion. (One might observe that, if this interpretation were sound, the Western decision to embark on the war with Germany, and moreover push it through to unconditional surrender, would be the wildest example of strategic wrong-headedness in human history.) But more moderate lines of argument dating the cold war from 1946 or 1947[10] and seeing it as stemming from Western reaction to Soviet wartime gains in Eastern and Central Europe, also contain in some instances an element of determination to cast the USSR as a victim. The debate here turns upon whether or not one defines the cold war as an essentially defensive engagement on the part of the West. It has obviously proved to be so on results: no single acre of established *Machtgebiet* has been lost to the Soviet Union as a consequence of the cold war, and one area still ambiguous in 1947, Czechoslovakia, did in fact fall to Soviet consolidation after the engagement began. One might, of course, argue that even though the West has in fact only maintained its power area, it had aspirations (war aims for the cold war) going well beyond this: aspirations variously described as ' liberation ' or ' rollback ' or ' negotiation from strength ', which looked to the reduction of Russia's power base in Eastern Europe by political if not military means. But these aspirations were at the level of velleity rather than will, even during the tenure of office of John Foster Dulles. He certainly talked a good deal about ' rollback ' during the Eisenhower election campaign of 1952, but, as one of his aides muttered on another occasion, you had to take everything Mr Dulles said with ' a whole warehouseful of salt '.[11] His declaratory policy was revisionist, but his operational policy was *status quo*, and this was made quite clear very shortly after he came into office, during the East German uprising of 1953. Thus to my mind the most reasonable judgement is that there has been no serious revisionism (in the sense that I used the term before concerning the Soviet Union of *willingness to take risks to secure change*) in Western policy *vis-à-vis*

[10] My own view is that conflicts should be defined on the basis of who the principal antagonists are, and that therefore dating the cold war from 1946 is quite reasonable: it is really just the name for the phase in international politics in which the chief antagonists are the USA and the USSR. There is no generally accepted name as yet for the new phase of triangular struggle including China.

[11] See Robert Murphy, *Diplomat among Warriors* (London, 1964), p. 470.

the Soviet sphere of power in Eastern Europe.[12]

One other factor ought to be mentioned as contributing to the early acceptance of the adversary relationship in the post-war as against the interwar period. That was the low level of utopianism in international politics. Such utopianism derives, to my mind, from an unconscious or unquestioned assumption that international harmony or co-operativeness, whatever content be given that notion, is the natural relationship between states, and that conflict is in some sense a deviation from normal. Clearly this is a view that owes very little to historical evidence, but in the immediate aftermath of the First World War, with the two dominant ideologies of international politics (those of Woodrow Wilson and Lenin) both anti-imperial, many people tended to put the endemic international conflicts of the past down to imperial ambition. The Versailles treaty was built on the notion that the nation-state was the ultimate, morally necessary, unit of political society. Once the national butterflies had emerged from the broken cocoons of the old empires, they might be expected to flutter peacefully together in the sunshine of democracy and collective security, in the new reformed international politics of the League. This expectation of the probability of peace, provided a few remaining grievances such as Germany's were redressed, did not receive many jolts until 1931 (the Japanese attack on Manchuria) or even 1935

---

[12] Many of those who have examined the cold war in the apparent hope of proving the opposite (of proving, that is, the cold war to be an aggressive rather than a defensive engagement for the West) seem to assume that some shocking sort of international immorality would be involved in such a project: implying that the Russians have some inherent natural moral right to sit on their neighbours, militarily and politically, if they find it convenient for their own security. Professor Graebner, for instance, writes of the ' primary Russian interest or right of hegemony in Eastern Europe ', and maintains that ' the Soviets claimed no more than the right to manage the political evolution of liberated Europe in terms of their own security interests.' (*Journal of Conflict Resolution*, Mar. 1969.) Quite so, but the Russian interpretation of ' their security interests ' includes all measures of military and political oppression needed to keep the other unfortunate peoples in their sphere of power in impotent subjection, as witness Czechoslovakia 1968–9. The West may have to acquiesce in this tyranny, but is not obliged to pretend that the tyrants have an unquestionable moral claim to do as they do. There is a tension in these matters between the claims of peace and the claims of justice, and while the claims of peace must be given priority, that is not to say that those of justice do not have any validity. See the author's *Negotiation from Strength* for a fuller account of Western aims in the cold war.

(the Italian attack on Ethiopia). Thus the immediate postwar experience was seventeen years of comparative international quiet, with its high point at Locarno. By contrast, there was no period which encouraged utopianism or assumptions of a natural harmony of interests after the Second World War. Even as the United Nations was being put together at San Francisco in 1945, the delegates received news of the Russian arrest of the Polish government-in-exile. There could not have been a clearer signal of Russian determination to hold in an unyielding grip the areas that its armies had occupied during the war. The peace had to be built on the necessary acceptance of injustice. The relevant concept was not to be that of a natural harmony of interests, but of a mode of living despite the sharp conflict of interests which had to be admitted.

Next in importance to this general acceptance of the adversary relationship was the fact that the balance of power was essentially bipolar from 1945 to 1962. In terms of crisis management this meant an unambiguous leadership of the *status quo* coalition. That is, whereas after 1918 leadership of the (unformulated) *status quo* coalition wavered uncertainly between two powers of roughly equal status, Britain and France, in the post-1945 period the difference in strength between the United States and the next power, Britain, was so great that no such ambiguity could arise for other powers. (There were a few groups in British politics, both on the far left and on the far right, who disputed the question of whether the *status quo* coalition as led by America was likely to serve Britain's true interests, as defined from their respective points of view. But they were not seriously influential after 1947, because they were far outweighed in policy formulation by the great bloc of ' centre ' opinion, comprising most of the Labour and most of the Conservative parties in parliament, who were reasonably happy with American leadership and policies, and sceptical of any suggestion that Britain could be leader of an alternative coalition, either Commonwealth or European ' Third Force '.)

This factor of a disparity in strength which rules out any ambiguity in leadership has a seamy side : it makes the prospect of what is usually called joint or allied crisis management rather a non-starter in most circumstances. (There are exceptions which will be looked at later.) But there is little doubt that, on balance, the existence of this disparity of strength, in obviating ambiguities of the sort that plagued Anglo-French joint leadership in the early interwar years, has been an enormous net advantage. Many people have complained of the inequalities in NATO: it is precisely because of those inequalities that it has survived more than twenty years. A partnership of fifteen truly equal powers would face intolerable problems of decision-making.

The unambiguous leadership and the bipolar balance are obviously closely related, but which should be regarded as cause, and which effect, is a moot point. Did the bipolar balance enforce the unambiguous leadership, by a kind of law of nature, or did the chance of unambiguous leadership create the bipolar balance? I am inclined to think that the latter may be the sounder view, and this becomes a problem of some interest as we come to consider the end of the bipolar balance. The world has been moving away from the relatively straightforward postwar situation since 1958, in a long transition which will not be complete until the mid-seventies. The emergent triangular balance of forces has some qualities ominously in common with that which existed during the crisis slide of 1936–9. Thus the question of whether unambiguous leadership can be maintained in a situation in which the balance is no longer bipolar is of more than academic interest. However, the experience of crisis management in the earlier bipolar and present transitional phases of the balance should be of value even in changed circumstances. Crisis management, as I said before, is learned behaviour, and it is not necessarily unlearned because the circumstances in which it needs to be exercised have changed.

The factors of difference that I have outlined seem to me the main impersonal reasons why the postwar period has so far produced no crisis slide of the sort one may discern in the final three or four years of the interwar period. But I am conscious that it might be argued that the true difference was simply one of personality, in that the postwar period has luckily thrown up no decision-maker for a major power who has consciously managed crisis towards war as Hitler undoubtedly did in some phases of the 1936–9 crisis slide. Nor have there been any two chief crisis managers as disastrously ill-matched as Hitler and Chamberlain: the pathological, visionary, political genius from the anti-semitic back streets of Vienna, and the decent, vain, limited Birmingham bourgeois who assumed that once the other man got a reasonable bargain he would be satisfied with it.

3

THE CONTEMPORARY CRISIS MANAGERS

DOUBTLESS it would be feasible, given sufficient historical know-ledge, to produce ' profiles ' of the sets of decision-makers who have managed international crises during each epoch of diplomatic history since 1815, and such a comparison might offer useful clues about the reasons for success or failure in the enterprise. But for this book all that is possible is some scrutiny of the major decision-makers of the postwar period in the role. Only for open societies can one gather much evidence of the influence of particular individuals in the decision-making process of this period, but even on our distant view of Chinese or Russian political processes one may receive some impression of the temperamental differences between Chou En-lai and Lin Piao, or between Khrushchev on the one hand and Stalin or Brezhnev on the other. The most useful comparisons, how-ever, are not primarily between individuals, but between the sets of intellectual influences which comprise the background mental furniture of particular policy-making élites. Thus one tends to use the names of the chief decision-makers in particular systems as a sort of shorthand, encapsulating a whole set of influences on the decision for which one or two men inherit the historical responsibility.

The attitudes I shall look at are, firstly, those of the three present dominant powers—the United States, the Soviet Union, and China; secondly those of their allies (major or minor); thirdly those of the non-aligned countries; and fourthly those of small powers who happen to be the focus of a particular crisis, and therefore may acquire a disproportionate share of influence on decision-making. It is of course the dominant powers who provide the chief decision-makers in crises of the central balance, but their allies may influence the management of such crises, and non-aligned powers such as India or Egypt may be the primary decision-makers in crises of local balances.

Of the three dominant powers, it is undoubtedly the Americans who find themselves least historically experienced in the diplomatic role concerned. I mentioned earlier Mr McNamara's remark, in the aftermath of the Cuba crisis, that there was no longer any such thing as strategy, only crisis management. That statement represented probably the earliest explicit definition by an American policy-maker of this as America's task in the world of powers. In fact the tight little group of self-conscious intellectuals round Kennedy was perhaps the first postwar American administration which could have defined it, even privately, in just that way. The policy-makers of the Truman and Eisenhower administrations had found themselves thrust out on the world stage in this role, and they had spoken the words and gone through the motions quite adequately, and even rather enjoyed it in some individual cases. But certainly Dulles would have had to define the task in different, more moralistic terms, and even Acheson would have hesitated, I think, to speak McNamara's formulation out loud. He might have seen things that way as Secretary of State, but Truman as President could not have accepted the formulation with as much nonchalance as Kennedy. This was because the dominant ideology of foreign policy in Washington, up to Kennedy's time, was one which rejected the concept of the world of powers as a system which needs to be managed by its chief members. The policy-makers adhered instead to various versions of an alternative doctrine, which has tended to see the society of states as the political equivalent of an Adam Smith economy, with the invisible hand of the natural harmony of interests ensuring that the system would regulate itself to the advantage of each member, provided they adhered to a few simple concepts like most-favoured-nation treaties and non-recognition of the fruits of aggression. The last completely wholehearted incarnation of this American world-view was Cordell Hull's policy in the thirties, but it has not even now been explicitly rejected by American Secretaries of State.

It is not surprising that Americans have shown less historical enthusiasm for the role of crisis managers than the European powers, since in the nineteenth century the US felt considerable apprehension (unjustified but persistent) as to what the Holy Alliance might undertake in that capacity in Latin America. The Monroe Doctrine is a testimony to the alarm the then president felt in 1823. Thus where the European chancelleries can look back on the Concert of Europe as their best period of extended crisis management—since it kept the peace for almost a century with only a few relatively non-catastrophic limited wars, even though it did break down by 1914,[1]—the Americans have mostly tended to see themselves as standing outside, and morally rejecting this tradition.

There was one earlier American president who could undoubtedly be described as an aspirant crisis manager for the world of powers, of great energy and ambition, though uncertain talent: Teddy Roosevelt. His interventions in the Russo-Japanese War and the Agadir crisis clearly show a strong, if premature, interest in the role for America. Later presidents, at least Woodrow Wilson and Franklin Roosevelt, also exercised the function, even though in the name of an ideology which rejected it. But Teddy Roosevelt's initiatives in crisis management were optional, and somewhat resented by the other powers; Woodrow Wilson's and F.D.R.'s, though necessary, were not seen as part of a system of permanent necessities; Truman's and Eisenhower's tended still to be viewed as temporary responses to extraordinary sets of circumstances. For American acceptance of the activity as a necessary, persisting, even normal part of a dominant power's role in a world where the formal machinery does not match the actual conflicts—for this one has to look as late as 1962. And this very recent acceptance of the role does imply a sense that it may yet again be rejected. The possibility of such a revulsion is one of the great uncertainties hanging over the present society of states. The disasters of Johnson's presidency (and perhaps Nixon's) have produced a dramatic loss of self-confidence among the American policy-making élite,[2] which could have far-reaching consequences in future attitudes, especially when one reflects on the degree to which the most intelligent American young have become alienated from the system and all its values. I can think of no historical equivalent of this: the

[1] The Franco-Prussian and Crimean wars were the chief counts against the system before 1914. The magnitude of the disaster of 1914–18 stemmed from other than diplomatic causes, including changes not then understood in the relationship between defensive and offensive technologies in warfare. The failure of military understanding produced the grim attrition of the trenches.

[2] The Pentagon papers may complete the devastation. Ironically, the archetypal member of this group, McNamara, had them gathered together, and a typical member, Daniel Ellsberg, used them against the establishment.

alienation of intelligent young people in the Britain of the thirties affected only a tiny minority by comparison.

It might be objected that China's experience in the role is even more recent than America's, if indeed it is conceded to have begun at all. But such a view of China neglects the enormous span of Chinese history before 1840, Chinese decision-makers up to then having been, in their own eyes and those of the other states within their orbit, the central managing élite of a complete world state, conferring legitimacy on lesser governments and arbitrating the quarrels between them. There is nothing in the Chinese traditional view of the world and their own role in it which is incompatible with the idea of crisis management.[3] Quite the reverse, in fact: it is a notion which would seem altogether natural to anyone versed in Chinese history, like Mao Tse-tung. Nor is this psychological influence at all weakened by the fact that the content of Chinese guidance for the peoples of the world outside China is now revolutionary. The messianic quality of Maoism must be regarded as the contemporary version of a traditional Chinese view of China's duty to supply moral and intellectual light to the dwellers in outer darkness.

I would, however, emphasize that the world has as yet no actual experience of Chinese policy-makers as crisis managers in the way that we have of the other two dominant powers, and we cannot really have such experience until the mid-1970s. This is because there has not yet existed, and will not until then exist, the strategic basis for an independent Chinese line on terms anywhere approaching equality with the other two. When one looks closely at a past crisis in which the ' adversary managers ' might seem, prima facie, to be Chinese, such as the Quemoy-Matsu crisis of 1958, one finds that the real strategic decision on which the outcome turned was Russian: the decision not to back China with nuclear weapons in any bid to regain the islands. The same is true of other Asian crises of the central balance, such as Indo-China 1954. It is only in local crises, such as that with India in 1962, that one can say that China has had a true strategic independence. Thus any

[3] See C. P. Fitzgerald, *The Chinese View of their Place in the World* (1964); or M. Loewe, *Imperial China* (1966).

analysis of China in the crisis-manager role must be drawn largely from doctrine and ' declaratory policy ', which is rather misleading, because the ' declaratory policy ' of any power tends to be somewhat fiercer and more intransigent than its ' operational policy '. This is certainly true of both the United States and the USSR.

With this reservation in mind, it is still possible to discern some influences on Chinese policy-making in crisis situations. Not much of what can be discerned is reassuring. There is, first of all, the fact that China has never been a full member of a society of states of the contemporary sort, or of any society of separate and equal sovereignties. Her two thousand years of historical experience before 1840 did not include the evolution of a system of diplomacy such as that which developed in the West, where the princes had to learn to take account of each other as self-willed equals. And in the century after 1840 she was undoubtedly a victim of, rather than a participant in, the Western society of states. The brief period of Roosevelt's sponsorship of Nationalist China as the major American ally, he hoped, in postwar Asia, left the present Chinese government that odd potential legacy, the formal status of a dominant power symbolized by permanent membership of the Security Council. But the conflicts from 1950 with the US have prevented the legacy being successfully claimed as yet, though it may be that the situation will change in 1971 or 1972, with American acquiescence.

This unique history of exclusion (and earlier self-exclusion) from the society of states means that Chinese historical experience and familiarity with modes of diplomatic behaviour is very restricted, compared with that of the other two dominant powers, and still more as compared to other crisis managers in earlier Western systems. This is important, because I shall be arguing later that communication is the main instrument of crisis management, and ability both to use and to *read* the finer nuances of diplomatic communication is a vital element in successful management. I am not by any means implying that the Chinese do not have a tradition of their own of ' esoteric communication ', conveying and reading messages between the lines. On the contrary, they have a painfully subtle and pervasive one, which enables the party cadres in Sinkiang to understand, for instance, that official publicity for a gift of mangoes from Mao to a particular faction in a university dispute should be interpreted as enabling them to get the local school children away from chanting cultural revolutionary slogans and out into the fields to gather the harvest. The point is that though the Chinese have this system of their own, they are not familiar participants in the Western tradition (which has become universalized), and that this impedes our interpretation of their crisis signals, as well as their receipt of ours. For instance, in the crisis period just before Chinese entry into the Korean war, the Chinese government certainly both sent a signal conveying the message ' we will march if . . . ' (sent via the Indian ambassador) and received a return signal intended to be reassuring (from Bevin, same channel). But neither seems to have been adequately interpreted.

Maoist doctrine is at best of ambiguous purport in this field. There is one maxim, ' Despise the enemy strategically, respect him tactically ', which certainly operates as a restraining guide, imposing prudence where the local balance of forces is unfavourable, and one may see the influence of this doctrine in a number of crises, including the final Chinese position in the Quemoy-Matsu crisis of 1958. But there is another Maoist tenet, which has been the central element of the Chinese dispute with Russia, which may be expressed as ' a single spark will *not* start a prairie fire ': that is, that the nuclear stalemate is complete enough to obviate any danger of people's wars touching off a nuclear Armageddon. This is held to indicate that people's wars can and should be vigorously pursued wherever the ground conditions make it possible. And it is the basis for the Chinese calling the Russians cowards because they hold, to the contrary, that people's wars, if too vigorously pursued, *could* lead to general nuclear war. If the Chinese really put as much faith in the blanketing effect of the nuclear stalemate as this particular doctrine implies, they would appear likely to be somewhat risk-taking crisis managers.[4] But this may be one of

---

[4] I am not implying that the Chinese are necessarily wrong in this judgement: on the evidence, they are quite probably right. It is nevertheless a discomforting doctrine to be held by a group of decision-makers in this league.

the instances when declaratory policy, as expressed at present, will turn out to be much more intransigent than operational policy.

One must add to these difficulties (comparative unfamiliarity with the modes of communication, and a doctrinal impetus to believe that the dangers are less than they appear, because Maoism is the wave of the future anyway and the historical fulfilment of its hopes is inevitable) a third factor which will be dealt with in more detail presently, but which is so important that it must be mentioned now: a comparatively low level of Chinese ability to gather intelligence in the West or—apparently —in Russia. I shall argue later that information about the other side's military capabilities and dispositions is an essential element in successful crisis management. The Chinese are beginning to enter this field, having put their first two satellites into space in 1970 and 1971, but for at least a decade there is likely to remain a persistent imbalance against them.

Thinking specifically about the management of crises between China and the Soviet Union (which have seemed since about 1967 to hold more likelihood of major war than those either between China and the United States or between the Soviet Union and the United States), one has to consider not only what the Chinese attitudes *are* but what the Russians *believe* about Chinese attitudes. If one took the Russians' own propaganda about China as evidence of what Russian decision-makers actually believe, one would have to say that the Russians are attributing to Chinese policy formulation a recklessness which few Western scholars would find there. The Russian pamphlet *The Nationalist Background of China's Foreign Policy*[5] attributes to Mao the statement, in 1959, that world politics should deliberately be maintained at a high level of tension: ' a superstition exists in some countries that international tension is unfavourable for the peoples. But in conditions of international tension the Communist Parties can develop more rapidly, the rate of development can be higher.' If this statement is authentically Mao's, it offers an interesting parallel with some of the attitudes of John Foster Dulles, who likewise

[5] By B. N. Zanegin, (1968).

maintained in some arguments with his allies (in his case during the approach to the 1955 summit) that a reduction in the level of world tension was *not* in the interests of world peace. In Mr Dulles's case, the argument was roughly to the effect that an adequately armed and united Western alliance could be maintained only while tension was reasonably high, and that therefore ' summitry ' whose chief effect was to reduce tension was contrary to Western interests, and might be productive of the miscalculations which precipitated war. One can make a case for this view of events, whether sponsored by Mao or Dulles, given the assumption of either that protracted conflict is the natural state of international politics at the present stage of human history. But a high level of tension will inevitably mean a high incidence of friction, so that a diplomacy based on this *Weltanschauung* must be expected to be unnervingly productive of crisis. Even if the viewpoint attributed to Mao does not represent either the reality of his outlook, nor yet the assessment by the chief Soviet decision-makers of what that outlook is, the fact that it has deliberately been given currency by the Russians indicates something of the modes in which the management of Sino-Soviet crises has proceeded since 1959.

As to Russia, one can say that adding up its Tsarist and its Soviet incarnations, it has certainly the longest recent historical experience in this role of any of the three present dominant powers. It is true that in both the Tsarist period and the interwar period, Russia was somewhat of an ' outsider ' among the powers, but never to such a degree as China or as—voluntarily —the US was for much of the nineteenth century. In the twenty-five years of the postwar period one can see a good many of the traditions of both the interwar (mainly Stalinist) and the Tsarist period asserting themselves. For instance, Soviet management of the intramural crisis of the Warsaw Pact occasioned by the political ferment in Hungary 1956 and Czechoslovakia 1968–9 vividly recalls Tsarist techniques in the same sort of situation in Poland or Finland in the nineteenth century.

It is difficult to sum up briefly so long an experience as that of Russian decision-makers in this field, but one might say that the tradition is normally cautious, but not at all skilful. If one is looking at Stalin's policy, for instance, either in 1939, or in 1938 at the time of Munich, or earlier in the Hitler period, it does not appear particularly successful in terms of the three criteria I have suggested for adversary crisis. As to the intra-mural crises with China in the period to 1962, on the evidence of results one would not be inclined to class them as skilfully managed. After all, in the upshot the alliance was ruptured, a discontented ally was turned into a dangerous enemy, and the intramural crises of the early period became the true adversary crises of the later period.

During Mr Khrushchev's time as chief decision-maker, one must conclude that Russian crisis management was on the whole much less cautious than under Stalin. The Chinese accusation of 'adventurism' in the Cuban missile crisis appears a perfectly reasonable judgement. Possibly also, though we do not know a great deal about his handling of the post-1957 portion of the intramural crisis with China, the same was true of that. Similar accusations of adventurism might be made of his conduct of Russian policy in the early period of the Congo crisis, and in the Berlin crisis of 1958–61. (The Berlin crisis of 1948, in Stalin's time, was far less an outcome of deliberate Russian challenge than that of 1958–61.)

One may put this down simply to Mr Khrushchev's own temperament, but it might have a different explanation. He was never, of course, anything like as secure in his position within the Russian oligarchy as Stalin, and he may have felt acutely the need for a big, spectacular success in foreign policy to strengthen his position vis-à-vis his potential rivals in the leadership. If he had ' brought off ' the Cuba effort, or alter-natively if he had ' brought off ' a big gain over Berlin in 1961, or even if he had managed a great ' peace-making ' success in the intended 1960 summit meeting with Eisenhower (which was actually ruined by the U-2 subcrisis) any of these might have helped him fend off his domestic critics. Again it is not possible to say how much the external failures weighed among the ' harebrained schemes ' which were given as the reason for his fall, but one can undoubtedly say that his successors have shown a marked return to Stalinist caution in the field of adversary crisis management, at least towards the West, if not towards the Chinese. In intramural crisis management (for example, Czechoslovakia) they have shown an entirely Stalinist ruthlessness.

The decision-makers of powers other than the dominant ones have roles in crisis management more or less proportioned to their ability to exert diplomatic or military leverage in the actual crisis situation concerned. Sometimes they can exact a kind of 'bonus' of influence above their real power by diplomatic skill or sheer intransigence: undoubtedly it is the French who have done best in this respect. However, all the allies of the United States, in its various systems of alliance, have had some influence on American crisis management of the particular regions with which they are concerned though in no case—except possibly Britain[6]—has the influence extended to all or most of such areas.

In fact the US range of alliance relationships is so extensive that one could use them as the basis for a study of whether, from the point of view of a minor power, membership of a bilateral or a multilateral alliance offers the best hope of maximizing its influence on the policy of the dominant power concerned during crisis. At first glance, one would be inclined to say that for minor powers the bilateral pattern offers the most scope, but that for major powers the multilateral pattern may be preferable. That is, if you compare the degree of influence exerted by a medium-small power like Australia, in a near-bilateral treaty (ANZUS) with that exerted by a medium-small power like Norway in a multilateral arrangement (NATO), you might conclude that the influence accruing to Australia was the more substantial. It is a matter of how many voices compete for a hearing by the dominant power at a given moment of crisis. In the Australian case one can say, I think, that there

---

[6] The pervasiveness of British influence on American policy is often underrated by those determined to prove that the 'special relationship' (of which this influence is a relic) has no longer any existence. It is true that the relationship is much weaker than it was at its peak, or plateau, probably 1941–56, but it is not true that it has altogether vanished. If one looks over the whole history of American policy in crisis situations, both adversary and intramural, from Azerbaijan in 1946 to 1970, the similarity of the lines taken by American and British policy-makers is very striking. There is one blazing exception to this, Suez, and a few smaller exceptions such as the Congo or Yemen.

has been in Canberra a definite feeling that the addition of Britain to ANZUS (the exclusion was originally much resented by Churchill) would have meant that the US would have had another voice, urging perhaps alternate priorities, to listen to in this particular forum in moments of crisis. That was probably true, though it should not necessarily be taken to mean that the British exclusion redounded as a whole to Australian advantage.

But if there is a tendency for small powers in a multilateral system to find their voices in crisis rather overlaid by those of other powers, the major powers in the same system may be benefited by the multilateral form. That is to say, in a case like NATO, the survival of the system as a whole is so valuable to the dominant power that the more essential major powers— Britain, France, and Germany in this case—have a larger influence jointly on the dominant power than any of them could have singly. In this special case there can therefore emerge something that more or less deserves the title of allied crisis management,[7] as for instance in the Berlin crisis of 1958–61. Berlin is a special case, even as crises within NATO are concerned, in that each of the four powers with troops there has an automatic military and political involvement, which enforces joint contingency planning and creates something like a basis for formal equality. But even here, the independent policy decisions of the United States, such as Kennedy's in 1961 concerning the calling-up of the reserve, may be the fulcrum on which the situation turns.

Other crises of the NATO area, such as Cyprus, have mostly seen rather less effective sharing of responsibility, and America's alliance systems other than NATO less yet. In the few cases where outside influence on American decision-making can be traced, there is sometimes a wry, back-handed quality to the results: for instance, Australian or Thai influence in some crises of the Vietnam war has not necessarily had the ultimate results that these powers intended.

Next there are the non-aligned powers. They may, of course,

---

[7] Often called *joint* crisis management, but I have avoided this usage because in fact many crises are managed ' jointly ' in the sense that at least two adversary powers are involved.

be primary decision-makers in the crisis of local balances, as India is in its crises with China or Pakistan, or Egypt in crises between Israel and the Arab world. In these cases their crisis management is often less restrained than that of the central-balance powers *vis-à-vis* each other. For one thing, the con-striction imposed by fear of escalation to the nuclear level is still absent in crises of local balances (save possibly that between India and China). However, since this study is mostly con-cerned with crises of the central balance, the major problem that we have to consider with respect to non-aligned countries is what influence, if any, they have had on crises in that sphere. I think the answer, in summary, is less than they hoped, less than they used to have, and less than that of aligned powers.

Undoubtedly, when Mr Nehru first enunciated his theory of non-alignment he hoped in effect, though he did not put it into these words, that the non-aligned countries would have a major influence on the crisis diplomacy of the powers of the central balance. The moral basis of the theory of non-align-ment was that it would not only be good for the security of the non-aligned powers, but good for the peace of the world. The way in which it was envisaged as operating was that the non-aligned countries would constitute a sort of ' floating vote ' in the argument between the dominant powers, bestowing their approval, on each individual issue, where the merits of the case lay. And this was expected actually to influence the behaviour of the dominant powers in crisis situations, because of the narrowness of the margin between them. Mr Nehru himself remarked, just before the Colombo conference of April 1954 ' When there is a substantial difference in the strength of the two opposing forces, we in Asia, with our limitations, will not be able to influence the issue. But when the two opposing forces are fairly evenly matched then it is possible to make our weight felt in the balance.'[8]

This was rather too parliamentary a vision ever to have had much relevance to the processes of international politics, but there was one crisis, that of 1954 over Indo-China, in which one can argue that the opinion of the non-aligned had a

[8] See the author's ' Non-Alignment and the Balance of Power ' reprinted in D. B. Bobrow, ed., *Components of Defense Policy* (Chicago, 1965).

substantial influence on the choices of the main decision-makers. This was really the peak period of the ' Bandung spirit ' even though Bandung itself was not until the following year. A thinner, more marginal, kind of influence on the part of this group of powers can perhaps be seen in the Suez crisis of 1956, and the Congo crisis of 1960, but hardly any trace is visible in most crises of the next decade.

Finally, we come to the special case of the influence on decision-making of those small powers which find themselves, reluctantly or willingly, the point of focus of a crisis between the powers of the central balance, like Cuba in 1962. How far have they the capacity to impose their wills on the dominant powers? Can they ' twist the arms ' of their great and powerful friends? Can Egypt determine the choices of the Soviet Union, Denmark or Norway those of the United States, Albania or North Korea those of China? I would on the whole argue that states other than the dominant powers have *less* influence on crisis situations nowadays than they had in earlier systems. This can be seen if one compares the comparative impotence of Cuba in the 1962 crisis with Poland in 1939 or Serbia in 1914. This declining leverage of minor (or even major) powers I put down to a factor that might be called great-power egotism, enforced by the nuclear age. In nothing are the three dominant powers more alike than in a steely determination not to permit their essential national interests to fall into the hands of minor (or even major) allies. The stakes are too high, in the nuclear age, for them to let anyone else call the bids.

This factor, to my mind, is a useful one from the point of view of preserving the peace (though of course it does not help to preserve the national interests of minor powers). There is an inherent probability that the minor powers in crisis situations will be the most intransigent,[9] because their interests will often be those most adversely affected, and they will be under a national compulsion to seek preservation of these interests even at a cost overwhelming in terms of the world as a whole, no matter what their own long-term price for such recalcitrance.

[9] Czechoslovakia in 1938 is a very marked exception to this rule: more intransigence on its part would in fact have benefited the management of that crisis.

One has only to think of the role played by Poland in 1939, in balking the agreement between Russia and the West which alone could, just possibly, have averted the Second World War, or the role of Serbian nationalism in precipitating the First World War.

It is difficult to imagine any power, even one as important as Germany, being as effective now as Poland was in 1939 in averting agreement between the dominant powers in the contemporary situation. Thus contemporary great-power egotism reduces the number of possible causes of central war by making it likely that the dominant powers will engage in major hostilities with each other only when they are convinced that their own vital interests are in danger, not to forward the interests of an ally. One can see this most clearly in the case of the Russian refusal to take risks to forward the national interests of China, in the matter of its regaining a bit of undoubted Chinese territory only a few miles off the coast, in the Quemoy-Matsu crisis of 1958. But one must also recognize it as the essential factor which has limited the leverage of Federal Germany within the NATO alliance, or specifically *vis-à-vis* the United States. Fears have been expressed in the West at regular intervals since 1950 that a Washington-Bonn axis might develop, in which the determining voice in policy-making towards the Soviet Union might be German. But such fears have always, in my view, been unrealistic, precisely because of this useful factor of great-power egotism. Looking back from the vantage point of 1971 over the twenty years for which Germany has been important to the Western alliance, one can see that at no time during that span was it important enough to enable it to use the leverage of the Western alliance to secure German national interests *vis-à-vis* the Soviet Union. And even the faint early possibility of this declined rather than increased as time went on, because of the way in which American risks in any such situation increased as Soviet capabilities grew.

Is it unfair to the minor powers involved in such situations to fear that, if they had diplomatic leverage enough, they would use it without adequate regard for the consequences? Not if one thinks of historical examples. A Serbian nationalist will still justify the Serbian nationalists of 1914 who brought their world, and everyone else's, crashing down about their ears. A Polish nationalist will still say that the Polish government had no alternative but to take the line it did concerning the Soviet Union in the negotiations of 1939. Dr Castro, in the crisis of 1962, would have forced Mr Khrushchev further towards the brink, if he had had the power.[10] It is probably inevitable that small oppressed nationalisms should take refuge in total intransigence when they are allowed to. But, luckily, contemporary circumstances seldom allow it.

The reverse problem to this is the question of how far the powers of the central balance can intervene in, or manipulate, crises of local balances. The classic instance here is Soviet machinations in various crises of the Arab-Israeli balance. Obviously the dominant powers do have the power to manipulate local balances if they are prepared to take the risks involved, but again I would tend to argue that they are less prepared to take these risks nowadays than historically has usually been the case. The risks are, firstly, an accidental encounter with another dominant power, and secondly, seeing your protégé make rather a mess of the situation, thus reducing your own prestige as a protector, or the prestige and even security of your weapons systems if they are incompetently used. (In the case of Soviet weapons in Egyptian hands, the Soviet high command is reported to have been more than a little enraged at their being captured by Israelis and presumably examined by Americans.)

It is inevitable that one should do some speculating about the psychological processes that produce good individual crisis managers. What qualities make for rational judgement in situations of great stress and immeasurable responsibility? In the final analysis the decision comes out of a face-to-face group of the President or the Prime Minister or the Party Chairman and a few of his closest advisers. As to relationships within this

[10] See the account given by the then British ambassador in Cuba, Sir Herbert Marchant, in the *Sunday Telegraph*, 15 Oct. 1967, also A. and R. Wohlstetter, *Controlling the Risks in Cuba* (London, Inst. for Strategic Studies, Adelphi papers, no. 17, 1965) for very convincing accounts of the attitude of the Cuban decision-makers at the time.

group, the outside observer has only the memoirs of those present as to whence came the most constructive or the coolest advice, and the memoir writers are naturally biased in favour of their own or their friends' roles. One can say that some political personages have shown an unexpected solidity, or even capacity for growth in moral and intellectual perceptiveness, under these almost intolerable pressures, and some have suffered a kind of shrivelling or distortion of their normal outlines. Robert and John Kennedy and Harold Macmillan seem to me examples of the first phenomenon, and President Johnson or Anthony Eden of the second. But the evidence on which one makes these judgements is admittedly thin, and might well be contested.

4

THE BASIS OF MANAGEMENT: THE ADVERSE PARTNERSHIP

HAVING looked to this extent at the actors in the contemporary diplomatic drama—the leads and the bit-players—we have now to consider the nature of the enterprise on which they are engaged: the basis, instruments, techniques, and conventions of crisis management. I distinguished earlier between adversary and intramural crises. The criteria of success in their management are different, but the modes by which it may be pursued are similar in a number of respects. One may examine, for instance, reasons for the success or failure of communications or intermediaries in either the one variety of crisis or the other. Even the use of armed force or the threat of force in their management is not totally dissimilar. Major hostilities are much more likely in adversary crisis, but intramural crisis may evoke minor hostilities. The Soviet Union used tanks in two of its intramural crises—Hungary and Czechoslovakia—and Cyprus, an intramural crisis for NATO, saw the use of air-strike by the Turks, and of small arms by both parties.

The difference between the use of armed force in crisis management and its use in war itself is the closeness of diplomatic control of the military measures. And this in turn arises from the limit imposed by the nature of the ends of military action. It is interesting that so perspicacious an observer as Carr could write, in 1939, ' In modern conditions, wars of limited objective have become almost as impossible as wars of limited liability.'[1] This is, for the postwar period, the precise contrary of the truth: in modern conditions it is *only* wars of limited objective and limited liability that have been found feasible. Indeed the postwar period may be characterized as a period of limited and peripheral wars. And this character of the time was becoming apparent by 1950, or even earlier. What factor was it that falsified Carr's observation, based on the history of the first forty years of the century, as it applied to the postwar epoch? The usual answer would be simply the invention of atomic weapons, but this seems to me altogether

[1] *The Twenty Years' Crisis*, p. 144.

inadequate. The limit on the objectives and liabilities undertaken in contemporary war has been more than a resolution to
avoid the use of nuclear weapons: it has included a restriction
of conventional war a long way below its all-out level as
demonstrated in the Second World War. I would suggest that
it has been a matter also of the development of consciousness
of a common interest in the limitation of hostilities to the level
of peripheral war and threatening gestures. The growth of this
consciousness can be traced right through the crisis history of
the postwar period from Azerbaijan in 1946: it produces what
I have called the conventions of crisis management, and at the
latter part of the period under review, perhaps after 1963, there
is a case for using the term ' adverse partnership '[2] to describe
the relationship it has induced between the dominant powers.
Or to be more precise, between two of the dominant powers,
the United States and the Soviet Union, since China was still,
in 1971, very much an outsider as regards this relationship.[3]
By ' adverse partnership ' I do not mean to imply anything
particularly cordial, trusting, or friendly: only a consciousness,
between the dominant powers, that they have solid common
interests as well as sharp conflicting interests. I would argue
that in this sense the central balance of power usually has been,
in Western diplomatic history, an adverse partnership, though
the level of consciousness of common interest has fluctuated a
great deal: very high during much of the nineteenth century,
for instance, and almost negligible during some stretches of the
twentieth century. Even at its highest it has never actually
ruled out the possibility of war between the parties. When that
stage is reached, one can regard the members of the grouping
as a ' security community ' of some sort, and crises between its
members would be intramural rather than adversary.

However, to revert to China's role as an outsider *vis-à-vis* the

[2] I owe this term to Professor Marshall Shulman.

[3] President Nixon's State of the World message 1971 contained a clear indication
that he (or Professor Kissinger) was becoming preoccupied with the impending
desirability of adopting China to it. ' It is a truism that an international order
cannot be secure if one of the major powers remains largely outside it and hostile
to it. In this decade therefore there will be no more important challenge than that
of drawing the People's Republic of China into a constructive relationship with
the world community. . . . We are prepared to establish a dialogue with Peking.'
The Times, 26 Feb. 1971.

relationship at present between the other two dominant powers, I would tend to argue that China's rise to the status of a dominant power has been one of the most important factors in the evolution of the sense of common interest between the other two. The consciousness (as between any set of dominant powers) that they have interests in common, is probably bound to rise and fall in the same measure as their consciousness of other dangers than each other. Thus one would expect it to be very low in periods when the power balance is seen as bipolar (as 1947–57) and to rise as this ceases to be the case. The situation of China as an increasingly formidable outsider is or was therefore a necessary condition for the initial trend towards the formulation of the adverse partnership, though in a later phase it may tend to seem desirable that China be adopted into it. To use a business analogy, one could think of the United States and the Soviet Union in the early part of the postwar period as rival power-brokers successfully absorbing their smaller competitors, and engaged in cut-throat rivalry with each other. There enters on this scene a third contender, China, whose presence at first makes it logical for the other two to move towards an informal cartel, the more successfully to resist the demands of the third claimant. But they cannot entirely hold this position, except at excessive costs to themselves. Once experience has shown this to be the case (experience as in Vietnam, for instance) then it becomes logical to think of extending the cartel to take in the third claimant—though this party's price for agreement may be very high, and the process of negotiating it will take a long time.[4]

Let us, however, return to the relationship between crisis management and this ' adverse partnership '. I think the relationship is circular, or perhaps spiral. That is, successful management of adversary crises helps create an adverse partnership, and this in turn makes the successful management of future crises more likely. But the powers could fall off this beneficent spiral at any moment, somehow losing their footing

---

[4] The Chinese would of course deny that any such possibility exists, but the denial is in itself evidence of their awareness of the possibility. See *Peking Review* 1 Jan. 1971: ' At no time will China ever behave like a superpower, neither today nor in the future.'

as the powers of an earlier central balance did in 1914. It took twenty-one years, from the Azerbaijan crisis in 1946 to the Middle Eastern crisis of 1967 for the present system to evolve, and a misunderstanding of its structure and dynamics could cause its fragile benefits to be lost almost overnight. The analyst must therefore try to discern what makes it workable. It seems to me that four main elements are apparent. I shall call them the exchange of hostages, surveillance, a common strategic ideology, and a bias towards preponderance of power on the side of the *status quo*.

The first element, the exchange of hostages, does not seem to require much examination since the idea is familiar to any-one acquainted with the general theory of deterrence. In an age of nuclear strike almost all the urban populations of each of the dominant powers and their allies may be regarded as ' hostages ' for the prudent decision-making of their respective govern-ments, in the sense that those governments have no way of protecting their peoples from the military sanctions available to the adversary power. This has been the case, in practical measure as the ' throw-power ' of the potential adversary has grown, for the populations of the USSR and Western Europe since the late 1940s, and the USA since 1958 or so. The date in each case is rather nominal, giving the starting point of a process rather than its point of true effectiveness.

Since the prospect of ABM systems began to look real in the mid-sixties, it has been argued that they might undermine this central prop of the deterrent system through allowing one side or the other to ' withdraw its hostages ' by providing effective defence for its city populations. Possibly if a highly effective system were available to one side, and no equivalent to the other, ABMs could seriously modify the present symmetry of deterrence as between the United States and the Soviet Union. But this does not really seem likely, since the two adversaries seem to have evolved systems that are roughly comparable. Given the level of research expenditure on each side and the diligence of intelligence services, some such comparability is perhaps probable in most kinds of advanced weapons systems. And provided that all that is in question is a reduction in the number of hostages on each side, no major modification of this element in the relationship seems likely. Seven million dead is probably as effectively deterring a prospect as seventy million. It may even be the case that this ' hostages ' factor works without any necessary comparability in the degree of damage each adversary is able to do the other. This is of importance in determining the leverage of China, whose ability to inflict damage on the other two is certainly far less (and will remain far less, even in the mid-seventies) than their respective abilities to inflict reciprocal damage. That is, even while the number of ' hostages ' held by China remains relatively low, the system may yet work for her as it does for the other two.

In the second relationship, surveillance, China is, as far as the available information goes, at a more serious disadvantage *vis-à-vis* the other two than in respect of the holding of hostages. But this is a field about which information is hard to come by, and it is possible that Western sources are underestimating Chinese capacities. By ' surveillance ' I mean simply the ability of the dominant powers to watch each other, to estimate each other's military capabilities, political intentions, and level of readiness. The traditional way of maintaining this watch has of course been by espionage. One would hesitate to assume that there has been any reduction in this branch of international endeavour: on the indications, it flourishes as robustly as ever. But the larger proportion of the special material that comes in to the ' intelligence community ' in the two dominant powers must certainly now be provided by the newer modes of scientific watching. (There is some slight indication that Britain and France also are beginning to operate in this field.) These systems rely on reconnaissance satellites, U-2 and similar aircraft, radar and sonar arrays, sensors on the sea-bed, upper-air analysis, seismographic monitoring of explosions, and techniques which are kept even more carefully secret than these. On such small fragments of information as are available to an outsider, one would assume that the whole land surface of each of the adversary powers is already under continuous photo-surveillance, at least weekly, to detect changes in military installations: China presumably receives this attention from each of the other two. The information so gathered relates primarily to capabilities, but some of it also says a good deal about intentions and ' readiness-posture ', for instance, the detected level of missile-alert.

Intelligence services, especially the CIA, have unhappily come to be used for other tasks than the gathering of information, but it remains their primary function, and there is a case for arguing that their contribution to the total flow of assessments which reaches decision-makers is of special importance. Ninety per cent of this total flow undoubtedly comes from the sources called ' white ' or legitimate. Governments deliberately convey to each other a great deal of perfectly genuine information about their respective capabilities and intentions. Speeches by political leaders; published arms budgets; parliamentary debates; demonstrations like the Soviet May Day reviews; official statistics; agreements on the presence of service attachés at embassies—all these provide a great deal of information deliberately made available to the adversary as well as allies and the home public. But since the relationship remains adversary, the very conveying of this information is within a framework which implies both the expectation and the reality of mistrust, deception, bluff, fraud, and guile. Each side must ask, totting up what has come in from these ' white ' or legitimate sources, not only *what* has the other side told us about its capabilities, but *why* have they told us this? Have they shown us a Potemkin village? This was very much the reaction in Washington after the first fly-past in the Moscow May Day parade of 1954 of the Soviet long-range heavy bombers, the Badger and Bison models. The Russians frequently describe the sort of inspection procedures proposed for arms control agreements as ' licensed espionage '. One could more reasonably describe espionage as unlicensed inspection, and useful (i.e. convincing) precisely because it is unlicensed. It derives its authority, like that of a Customs ' random check ', from the fact that no volunteering is involved on the part of those subject to check. (Detecting the cases where there is such a ' volunteering ', e.g. through a double agent, is of course a notable element in the art of transmitting only authentic information to the chief decision-makers.)

Precise knowledge of the military capabilities of the adversary power, and preferably of all the powers concerned in a given crisis, is obviously useful to the success of its management. Compared to the thirties, we are now literally in an age of surveillance in which the disguise or underrating or overrating of military capabilities at least by the dominant powers is much less likely than before. It remains true that intention is much harder to establish than capability; however, since, in the past, judgements of capability have been fully as much in error as judgements of intention, at least one of the factors which produce miscalculation has been reduced. As I said, even intention is somewhat 'visible' in the age of surveillance. Various indices which are regularly monitored, such as the degree of missile alert and aircraft dispersion, signal intention (or expectation) as well as capability. During the Cuban missile crisis, for instance, the CIA was able to determine that the Russians had not ordered a full missile alert, and this was a useful restraining influence in American decision-making.

(There is a nice illustration in the Cuban missile crisis of the interrelation between intelligence gathered by traditional espionage and that derived from contemporary modes of surveillance. The primary information on the missiles was secured, as everyone knows, from photo-reconnaissance by U-2 overflights. But the information which enabled the CIA to deduce that the first small and indefinite indications on the photographs from Cuba were for IRBM installations had been supplied by Colonel Penkovsky—figures for dimensions of particular kinds of missiles and such. He is also said to have been the chief source for the information that the state of the Russian nuclear armoury was such that Mr Khrushchev must back down, given a direct challenge. But this I regard as more doubtful, because that estimate (and it could never be *more* than an estimate) must have rested on information from many sources.

One may compare this situation with that arising during the three-handed involvement (the West, the Axis, and the Soviet Union) in the crisis slide which ended in the Second World War. There were reasons on both sides for the failure of the negotiations between the West and the Russians, and the strongest of these reasons was undoubtedly Stalin's decision to

opt for the short-term advantages of the alliance with Hitler.[5]
But the low level of Western enthusiasm for the Soviet alliance
was a large contributing factor, and this in turn resulted largely
from a serious underestimation of Russian military strength.
Mr Chamberlain, for instance, could write:

> I have no belief whatever in her [Russia's] ability to maintain an
> effective offensive, even if she wanted to. And I distrust her motives,
> which seem to me to have little connection with our ideas of liberty,
> and to be concerned only with getting everyone else by the ears.
> Moreover, she is both hated and suspected by many of the smaller
> states, notably by Poland, Rumania, and Finland.[6]

Today's policy-makers could echo with even better evidence
Chamberlain's judgement that Russian policy had nothing to
do with Western notions of liberty, and could add that the
small states in her ambit have been shown to have good reasons
to fear and suspect her. (Those who sup with the Russians as
allies have needed uncommonly long spoons.) The error which
would now be less likely is in the strategic appreciation of
Russian military capacity. Chamberlain's views on this matter
were not peculiar to him alone: as Medlicott has pointed out,
the general diplomatic estimate was to the same effect. The
British Embassy in Moscow, including the service attachés,
were steadily pessimistic as to Russian strength and willingness
to co-operate with the West, through the Sudeten crisis period
as well as in 1939.[7] Again one can understand this: the Russian
armed forces really were in some respects weak in offensive
strength. As Stalin himself admitted, they made a poor showing
in the war against Finland. What was overlooked in the estimates, and was to prove of inestimable importance, was what
Stalin later called the ' permanently operating factors ' which

[5] On the basis that agreement with Hitler offered at least temporary exemption
from the coming war, whereas an alliance with the Western powers meant immediate involvement in any such war. Also the British guarantee to Poland and
Rumania meant that the West was committed in any case to such efforts as it
could make towards blocking German expansion in that direction, which in effect
provided Russia with a sort of Western-sponsored buffer zone, without its making
any diplomatic payment for it. But of course the *costs* to Russia of the accretion
to German strength by the conquest of Eastern Europe proved much greater than
the *benefits* (if any) of a few months longer to prepare for the war.

[6] K. G. Feiling, *The Life of Neville Chamberlain* (1946), p. 403.

[7] See ' The Coming of War in 1939 ' in Medlicott, ed., *From Metternich to Hitler.*

enabled the Russians to absorb the German attack, and ultimately to break the German armies on the Eastern Front.

The underestimate of Russian military capacity over the long
haul was paralleled by an overestimate of the effectiveness of
German forces in being, especially the Luftwaffe. Both Jodl
and Keitel after the war gave evidence that during the crisis
slide of 1938–9 German military strength was much less substantial than it was taken to be by Western decision-makers.
Jodl said at Nuremberg that if the Western powers had stiffened
themselves to the point of war during the Czech crisis, Germany
would have suffered an immediate defeat.[8]

It would be much too optimistic to assume that the age of
surveillance (which was fully set up only in 1962) has eliminated
the possibility of disastrous misjudgements of military capacity.
Anyone who has looked at the connection between political
decision-making in crisis situations and the material supplied
to the decision-maker by the intelligence community will have
been struck by a curious kink or disparity between them. Often,
as before Pearl Harbour, the decisions seem to have been taken
in the teeth of the evidence. A practitioner in the field once
told me that this is because intelligence communities have a
tendency to ' hedge their bets ', like fortune-tellers, putting up
interpretations which can be read more than one way. Still, it
seems reasonable to assume that the margin for error has now
been reduced, though even the most perceptive modes of
surveillance will never eliminate it completely. One cannot
regard the debate over the ' missile gap ' in the United States,
in 1959, as disproving these assumptions about the new techniques. For one thing, that debate was largely a piece of
shrewd electioneering on the part of hopeful Democrats, and

[8] The military strength of the powers involved—Germany, Czechoslovakia,
Britain, France, and Russia—which affected management of the Munich crisis is
too involved a subject to be explored here. The German high command may have
been so convinced of Germany's military weakness that they would have mounted
a *coup* against Hitler rather than let him press demands to the point of war. The
British Chiefs of Staff were equally pessimistic about British armed forces, especially
capacity for air-defence. See a long correspondence in *The Times* in Aug. 1970.

The Pentagon papers offer a striking illustration of the limits of the intelligence
community's influence on policy. CIA estimates on such matters as Hanoi's ability
to withstand US bombing were quite realistic—and quite disregarded by the
Washington decision-makers.

for another the real technological developments necessary only date from 1962, as far as effective deployment is concerned.

The age of surveillance also eliminates from the dominant powers' attitudes *vis-à-vis* each other a very dangerous element: the hope of achieving strategic surprise. Here we must distinguish between three problems: the question of whether one particular power *can* achieve strategic surprise against another; the question of whether the decision-makers of either party *believe* they can achieve such surprise; and the question of whether they believe such surprise will be *effective*.

Obviously, some powers can still hope for this against some others, in local balances, and it has stood them militarily in very good stead. The Israeli air force seems to have achieved almost total strategic surprise against the Egyptians in the Six Day war of 1967, and in effect this won the war for them. The Chinese seem to have achieved very substantial strategic surprise against the Indian army in 1962, and again it stood them in very good stead. The Russians may have achieved tactical surprise over Czechoslovakia in 1968, though I am rather doubtful whether they sought it, since on the whole it would have been more dangerous to them that NATO should *not* know their intentions (and thus possibly misconstrue them) than that it should.[9] But it seems clear that the belief that one might achieve strategic surprise could be a dangerous temptation to decision-makers in crisis, and one must therefore regard the great invisible net of surveillance which the decision-makers of the dominant powers maintain *vis-à-vis* each other, *and know to enmesh themselves*, as a factor making for prudence.

This point seems to me so important that I will spell it out further. It is not only the decision-maker's knowledge that he has an effective surveillance over the adversary, but equally the assumption of a similar level of such knowledge on the other side, that permits the necessary confidence to grow in the *predictability* of the adversary and the reliability of his signals. If the decision-makers of the United States, for instance, had

---

[9] Lord Chalfont, then Minister of State at the Foreign Office, has revealed that he was in fact woken in the middle of the night to be given official advice by the Russian Ambassador in London of the Russian move into Czechoslovakia. *New Statesman*, 27 Nov. 1970.

to take into account the possibility that Soviet decision-makers might be wildly wrong about American capabilities, it would add a destructive element of radical uncertainty to their calculations.

The other variety of information which has been the chief preoccupation of intelligence services in the nuclear age has been early warning of notable break-through in scientific research. Its transmission has had a quite different, but equally important function in the growth of the adverse partnership. It has helped account for the increasing symmetry of weapons systems on the two sides of the balance. I suppose this symmetry would in due course have emerged even without the services, to put it delicately, of people like Klaus Fuchs and the others, but it would not have begun to emerge as early as it actually did, that is by 1949, with the testing of the first Soviet atomic device.

It is this symmetry of the weapons structures of the two dominant powers which in turn permitted the evolution of the next factor in the adverse partnership, which I have called a common strategic ideology.[10] I do not by this mean to imply that American and Soviet assessments and theories are alike on all points in the strategic field. On the contrary they have differed a good deal on various matters. What I mean is that their overall general appreciation of the nature of the new weapons has grown steadily more similar since 1953, when Stalin's death permitted the junking of his orthodoxy of the ' permanently operating factors '. If this proposition seems doubtful, consider what the intellectual basis of the Strategic Arms Limitation Talks could be if not a tacit consensus as to the meaning of these weapons.

The two parties have to assign roughly the same meaning to particular weapons, have to see the potential battle to some extent in the same terms, to be able to negotiate meaningfully about it, or even to believe that negotiation between themselves might be useful. The evidence that this is the case is not to be looked for in words: the ' declaratory policies ' of the two adversaries may well remain quite distinctive, especially on

[10] I owe this term to Professor Hedley Bull; see his ' Strategic Studies and its Critics ', *World Politics*, July 1968.

points like whether limited war is possible, and the feasibility of use of tactical nuclear weapons. The evidence of the ' operational ' strategic ideology, as against the declaratory one, is to be found in the structure of the armed forces which the decision-makers have chosen to make available for their future selves. The reshaping of Soviet military programmes since Mr Khrushchev's time has patterned itself quite clearly on the American model, not only in the initial shift towards a nuclear deterrent force, but in the later emphasis on mobile forces suitable for use in local crises. Thus the build-up of Soviet naval forces, for instance, must undoubtedly be related to Soviet observation of how useful such forces were to the United States in the Lebanon-Jordan crisis of 1958 and the Cuban missile crisis of 1962.

It will be objected that this sort of tacit understanding within a limited specific field is not what most people mean by an ideology. The word usually is reserved in the loose Western usage for a system of general ideas about the political, cultural, and economic relationships of a society, or else, in the Marxist usage, for the ' false consciousness ' of a particular group, rationalizing the situation of advantage or disadvantage in which that group finds itself. From the point of view of the great nuclear dissident, China, the common American and Soviet system of ideas is of course seen in the latter fashion as a rationalization of the situation of nuclear advantage in which the United States and the Soviet Union find themselves. But from a Western point of view it may be interpreted as a ' special ideology ' as against a ' general ideology '[11]—that is, an ideology special to a particular professional group. And here there is a striking parallel with the society of states of the nineteenth century. The differences in domestic political ideologies between the powers of the Concert of Europe period seemed hardly less great to the men of that time than did those between Mr Brezhnev's Russia and Mr Nixon's America in 1971: perhaps more so. But the diplomatic relations of the epoch were controlled by a small group at the top of each society, who shared a considerable stock of common concepts

[11] See Karl Mannhein, *Ideology and Utopia* (London, 1960) for a general discussion of these concepts.

and values (those of an international aristocracy) with their
opposite numbers in the other dominant powers. In fact this
similarity was so great that individual members of those élites
could choose in which service to make their careers, without
undue attention to national origins: one of the German gentry
like Nesselrode could be the chief foreign policy decision-maker
for Tsarist Russia. I suppose the nearest contemporary equivalents would be the displaced intellectuals of German birth who
have entered the American service—a Von Braun, a Kissinger,
and so on. But the point now is the mobility of ideas rather
than of individuals. The strategic theorists of the nuclear age,
practically all Americans, provide their theoretical services
equally to the adversary, whether they wish to or not, simply
by publishing and teaching. Usually there is a lapse of five
years or so before the transfer of ideas is visible. But if you ask
who is the Soviet version of Schelling or Kahn or Wohlstetter,
the answer is probably Schelling or Kahn or Wohlstetter, even
though the doctrine may be mediated through Sokolovsky or
Talensky or Rotmistrov.[12]

Obviously this special professional ideology, built around the
military means of the nuclear age, is never likely to extend
much beyond a tiny élite of policy advisers. But probably
international ideologies never *have* extended much beyond a
very small minority. They remain effective so long as the
decision-makers share them, and as the Chinese are fond of
pointing out, this has clearly been the case as between American
and Russian decision-makers in a number of crises since about
1958.

(I will not here deal with the present Chinese rejection of, or
exclusion from, this strategic ideology, except to say that it may
be related to, among other things, the Chinese disadvantage
in the field of surveillance. If you look at the differences over
strategy between China and the Soviet Union in a number of
crises from 1958 to 1962—differences which were great enough
effectively to destroy the Sino-Soviet alliance—you can say that

[12] The gathering of information and techniques would seem now to be quite
conscious and organized as far as the Russians are concerned: for instance, a
notable Western exponent of the crisis-game technique has been ' borrowed ' for
a game in Moscow, and there have been other Russian indications of interest at
the political rather than the academic level of interest in crisis theory.

they comprised a number of factors, the most important perhaps being asymmetry of national interests, but there is a
perfectly clear element of less understanding on the Chinese
side of the realities of American will, and even capability.
This must be related to the Chinese disadvantage in surveillance
techniques.)

Former high officials of the Department of State are now
able to acknowledge how radically the American international
ideology has changed, as witness George Ball:

No one can seriously contend that we now live under a universal
system or, in any realistic sense, under the 'rule of law'. We maintain the peace by preserving a precarious balance of power between
ourselves and the Soviet Union—a process we used to call ' contain-
ment' before the word went out of style. It is the preservation of
that balance which, regardless of how we express it, is the central
guiding principle of American foreign policy. . . . Not only do we
still depend on the time-honored device of the balance of power,
which both the League of Nations and the United Nations were
supposed to render obsolete, but we tacitly claim and recognize
other hoary concepts as, for example, ' spheres of influence' or,
more accurately, ' spheres of interest'. We paid deference to such
a Soviet sphere in 1956, when we sat by while Russian tanks
rolled into Budapest. . . . For their part the Soviets tacitly acknowledged our sphere of interest when they stood by while we sent the
marines and paratroopers into the Dominican Republic in 1965. . . .
All but the wildly romantic are agreed that we will never be able to
achieve a workable universal system until the two global powers are
prepared to follow parallel, if not common, lines of action on a
reasonably broad spectrum of policies.[13]

It would be unrealistic to expect a Soviet policy-maker, or
ex-policy-maker, to be equally candid in declaratory policy,
but I believe that Soviet operational policy, judged against
Leninist doctrine in 1917, has moved as far as American policy,
judged against Woodrow Wilson's doctrines in 1917, and in the
same direction: towards an ideology which uses something like
the justifications (as well as the techniques) of the traditional
European system, but on a world scale. *Strategic* ideology is the
growing point, to my mind, for the general international
ideology, because it derives from the interests which the

[13] *Foreign Affairs*, July 1969, pp. 624–5.

dominant powers have in common. Other items of ideology emphasize the issues on which they are at odds, or else are neutral, like the concept of sovereignty.

If you look at the actual growth of formal treaties (as against tacit agreements) between the dominant powers this becomes quite evident. The two chief milestones of the process were the Partial Test Ban Treaty of 1963, and the Non-Proliferation Treaty of 1968, both indisputably outgrowths of the common strategic ideology, evolved in the USA and adopted in the Soviet Union. Both treaties naturally are the objects of furious attack by the ' outsider ' member of the future group of three dominant powers, China. When China begins to see some merit in those two treaties, one will know that it is at last a full member of the nuclear dominant powers club, and beginning to adhere to the American-Russian strategic ideology.

This brings us to the point of considering whether Chinese exclusion, or self-exclusion, from the strategic ideology at present (and indeed its dissent from practically the whole ideological structure which supplies such consensus as exists in the present society of states) vitiates the usefulness of this ideology as one of the crucial bases of crisis management. The answer, I think, is that over the transition period in which the other two powers—either singly or combined—are vastly stronger than China, this Chinese dissent is not necessarily fatal. Beyond that transition period we must hope, and may expect, that China will adopt some at least of the propositions of the strategic ideology.[14]

As I said in the last chapter, we have as yet no actual experience of China as an equal partner in this field. Nor have we had much experience in the postwar period of crisis as a three-handed game.[15] But the world did experience such a situation in the latter part of the interwar period, and it was

[14] The Chinese, as I mentioned on p. 51, must and do of course claim that this will never happen, since it would amount to revisionism. This is their only possible ideological arguing position at the moment, but it is not necessarily a true prognosis. For a fuller account of their attitude on this issue see C. P. Fitzgerald in C. Holbraad, ed., *Super-Powers and World Order* (Canberra, 1971).

[15] Even the mathematical techniques which deal with conflict rather than crisis are mostly preoccupied, in the jargon, with two-person, zero-sum games. As someone has noted, the ' two persons ' are assumed to be identical twins, thinking like American conflict strategists.

undoubtedly very dangerous and disastrous. It would be craven to avoid noting the parallel between the triangular balance of forces of 1936–9—the West, the Axis, and Russia—and the triangular balances of forces impending from about 1976—the West, China, and Russia. Is there something inherently unstable in triangular balances?

It would be too pessimistic to assume this was necessarily the case, but one must concede that a triangular balance tends to give greatest scope for apprehensions of the possibility which I shall call collusion. (I choose this word deliberately, rather than a blander term like ' co-operation ' or ' tactical shift of alliance ' because I think that it conveys moral ambiguities which ought to be admitted, and also because I want to use analogies with certain past episodes which can be so described.) That is to say, the impending triangle of forces must not be thought of as necessarily a stable equilateral triangle, with the points always or even usually the same distance apart. It is a triangle with adjustable sides, so that any two of the points may be man-oeuvred together (at least temporarily) at the expense of the third. And this introduces a factor which might be expressed in a rather cynical-sounding maxim: there is probably a big future for collusion. Any comprehensive handbook of crisis management for policy-makers could hardly avoid including a chapter entitled ' How to collude with an adversary without actually mistaking him for a friend '.

For each of the three dominant powers, the most dangerous and disadvantageous situation is that produced by the collusion of the other two. One can see a preoccupation with this fact already in each of the three countries. The Chinese are the most apprehensive: the *Peking Review* every week harps on the collusion between the ' imperialists ' and the ' social imperia-lists ' (as it now likes to call the Russians in order to play up the parallels between the policies of the two powers in the ' Third World '). This preoccupation is sometimes carried to rather comical lengths, as in the Chinese interpretation of the visit of the American astronaut Frank Borman to Russia. He was received by President Podgorny, who remarked as the television lights were switched on, ' This room was cold, but now it is getting warmer.' Just the rather desperate small-talk of such occasions? Not to the *New China News Agency*, which disclosed that this feeble conversational gambit ' clearly revealed the Soviet revisionist renegade clique's intention of moving towards still closer collusion with American imperialism. '

The Chinese preoccupation with ' collusion ' is more audible than that of the other two dominant powers, because for reasons which will be explored, the danger is most real in their case. But it may also be seen in the other two dominant powers. In Washington it now chiefly takes the form of speculation on the post-Mao situation in China, with for instance Chou En-lai and forces associated with the army possibly working to put the Sino-Soviet alliance back together, mostly for the necessities of military procurement. In Russian official reactions, one can see the preoccupation especially in the nervousness on the occasions when the Warsaw talks actually take place between Americans and Chinese, and in their taunting the Chinese with such agreements as these talks produce (for instance, the agreement about the limits of American bombing in Vietnam).[16]

One side effect of the apprehension of collusion between any two of the dominant powers as the most daunting prospect for the third (whichever that should be) is that each of the three powers ought logically to have a ' preferred area of crisis '. That is, it is not difficult to discern that there are particular areas in which crises are most effective in diminishing the prospect of collusion between any two of the powers, and this area ought logically for the third power to be its ' preferred area of crisis ', i.e. the area which most conveniently diminishes the greatest single danger that it may theoretically face: the ganging-up of the other two against it.

Thus one might argue, for instance, that for China the ' preferred area of crisis ' should be Eastern Europe, because this is the area in which Russia and the Western powers are each most sensitive to even small changes in the power balance, and where frictions most readily set back the *détente* (or as the Chinese would call it, the collusion) between the USA and the USSR. (The Chinese have sometimes used a single expression for these

[16] Professor Allen Whiting has given some details which add colour to the Russian allegations on this; see *Life*, Mar. 1969.

two powers: the USSA.) In the light of this analysis one would expect some Chinese welcome and encouragement for Czech-type events, and this explains what might otherwise seem ideologically puzzling: the strong Chinese support for the Czechs in 1968–9. From a Maoist eye-view the Czechs had gone even further down the bourgeois-revisionist path than the Russians, of course. Nevertheless the *Peking Review* came out strongly in support of Mr Dubcek. There are some curious corollaries of this Chinese interest in Eastern Europe. China manoeuvres with Rumania, which has the merit of being domestically Stalinist as well as diplomatically and economically restive in the Russian sphere. And it cultivated an acquaintanceship (and a high level of trade) with West Germany, at least until the Russo-German *rapprochement* of late 1970, which naturally attracted a bitter denunciation in Peking.[17] A hope in Peking for a tactical co-belligerent in Bonn was not so wildly unreasonable as it may now seem: each had a strong interest against the stability of Russian hegemony in Eastern Europe, Bonn for obvious reasons, China because unrest there harasses the Russian power-base at its most sensitive point, reduces the moral ease of collusion with the Western powers, and distracts Russian attention from its Far Eastern frontier.

From the Russian point of view the preferred area of crisis, the one most likely to prevent any collusion between the United States and China must undoubtedly be East Asia and South Asia. A re-run of the Quemoy-Matsu crisis, a larger crisis over Taiwan, or Hong Kong (as to which Mr Khrushchev himself reproached the Chinese with acquiescence in imperialist control): any of these would be calculated to blight such small shoots of effort towards better understanding between China and the US as have been allowed to develop. Korea is a more uncertain case, perhaps because it would be a very large and dangerous crisis, perhaps because it is close to vulnerable Russian territory at Vladivostok. South Asia, on the other hand, especially the Indian border area, offers a kind of bonus pay-off for Russian crisis management, in the sense that Chinese adventures here not only minimize prospects of easier relations between China and America, but provide a basis for positive

[17] See *Peking Review*, 18 Sept. 1970.

collaboration between Russia and America. This has been true since the 1962 crisis on the China-India border, which began the supply of arms by both countries to India, and the Tashkent Agreement, which was crisis management by Russia with the clear blessing of the United States.

For the West, I suppose it might be argued that the most convenient area of crisis is the Amur-Ussuri-Mongolia-Sinkiang area, in the sense that the repeated clashes over territorial points in this remote wasteland have undoubtedly further reduced what slight prospect there may have been for restored collaboration between China and Russia. That is *not* to say that it would be to Western interests that these endemic crises should be mismanaged into major hostilities. Major hostilities between any two nuclear powers hold unpredictable dangers for the whole world. Indeed, crises in this area might prove especially dangerous to the world as a whole because there is so little scope for outside leverage on either of the two sets of decision-makers. The only power with any such leverage would be the American government: its intervention could be so fateful for either that one would assume that either China or Russia, if contemplating major hostilities, would send out signals to ascertain the American attitude. (An excessively Machiavellian approach to the prospects of collusion might, for instance, argue that the only situation in which the Soviet Union could conceivably bargain away such a substantial asset as its control of East Germany would be one in which it needed Western support against China.)

The Chinese assumption that the likeliest possibilities of collusion are between the United States and the Soviet Union can be as readily reached from a traditional power-political analysis as from a Maoist one. Both the United States and the Soviet Union are endowed with the primary interests of *status quo* powers (though the Soviet Union does not talk like one) with more to gain from maintaining the present structure of power in the world than from upsetting it. Indeed, it would be very surprising if a state as advantageously placed as the Soviet Union in the share-out of power and territory in the world were interested in overall change, *at least where this entailed any serious element of risk.*

There are certainly areas of the world, specifically South Asia and the Indian Ocean, where the Russians seem at present strongly interested in increasing their influence, but these are areas with a low present risk of collision with the United States. In any collision with China, or for that matter minor powers like Britain, India, and Australia, the Soviet Union will be in a position of considerable advantage, especially after the Suez Canal is reopened. What is more, if the Guam doctrine means what it seems to mean in American foreign policy, this area will continue to be one of potential low-risk, low-cost gains for the Soviet Union. Russian policy might be defined as pursuit of the spoils of opportunity, and anyone familiar with the imperial history of the nineteenth century will observe it with a sense of *déjà vu*, especially in contemplating the role of the gunboat, from the *Pax Britannica* to the *Pax Sovietica*. But this highly traditional turn in Soviet policy is not incompatible with maintenance of its predominantly *status quo* interests in the central triangle of forces.

China, on the other hand, may be interpreted as a true revisionist power, with incentives of every sort—ideology, redress of past national injury, economic disadvantage, population pressure—for seeking overall change in the structure of power in the world. And these incentives are, at least at present, quite open and undisguised in Chinese policy. Thus the prospects of collusion, even in the way of temporary informal tactical alliance between China and either of the other two seems quite remote and difficult to envisage. China may of course find tactical allies, from among powers dissatisfied with a local *status quo*: let us say some Arabs in the Middle East, or Rumania in Eastern Europe, or conceivably France in Western Europe, or Pakistan (regime rather than dissidents) in South Asia, or various as yet unforeseeable states in Africa and Latin America. But it is unlikely to be able to effect even a temporary collusion with either of the two dominant powers, since they have too much to lose from its growth in strength.

Thus one may on the whole say that preponderant power, for a long time to come, is likely to rest with the tacit *status quo* understanding between the USA and the Soviet Union. And this I regard as a condition conducive to peace. It is not a *balance* of power (in the sense of an equality) which preserves peace: it is a solid preponderance of power on the side of the *status quo* coalition, formal or informal. The long European peace (or near-peace) of the nineteenth century reflected such a situation, until the rise of Germany began to disturb it. The onset of the First World War occurred during a period of fairly even balance, France-Britain-Russia versus Germany-Austria with Italy ambiguous and the United States non-aligned. The only firm adherents of the *status quo* of the Versailles settlement, Britain and France, could not muster much of a margin over the revisionists—Germany, Italy, and Japan—after 1934. More important, they did not look as if they wanted to. The Soviet Union wavered ambiguously between a *status quo* and a revisionist position until 1939, when Stalin made his temporary tactical alliance (or collusion) with Hitler in the Nazi-Soviet pact. And that bad piece of Russian crisis management provided the condition of temporary strategic advantage to the revisionist coalition which in turn precipitated the war.

Perhaps the most important single difference between the triangular balance of the interwar period and the prospective triangular balance of the seventies and eighties, America-Russia-China, is that it is difficult to believe in any sudden future shift of preponderant power to the revisionist camp, similar to that which operated for the period August 1939–June 1941, the period of the Nazi-Soviet pact. It is true that, as I said, for both periods Russia may be construed as having wavered ambiguously between a *status quo* and a revisionist position, and that one might therefore argue that, just as the chief Russian decision-maker in 1939 assumed it would be of temporary tactical advantage to Russia to opt for the revisionist camp, some future Russian decision-maker might come to the same conclusion, and a parallel agreement to that of August 1939 might produce the same kind of cataclysm, forty years or so on. Luckily history does not usually repeat itself in quite so simple-minded a fashion.

These are the true bases of contemporary crisis management, as I see it: the exchange of hostages, the growth of surveillance, the elements of a common strategic ideology, and the fact that in the present triangular balance of forces there is a show of preponderant power on the side of the *status quo*. But if these are the foundations, there is something that might be regarded as a kind of rough flooring laid across them to make manoeuvre easier, and that is the *détente*. I am not sure one needs to define *détente* any more exactly than as the reduction (not ending) of tension between the dominant powers. Note that it is the dominant powers' attitudes to each other that are important for the purposes of general crisis management, and not the attitudes of their local allies. For instance, the Soviet Union's invasion of Czechoslovakia severely damaged the *détente* between the European members of NATO and the Warsaw Pact, and set back East-West co-operation in Europe. But it hardly damaged the American-Soviet *détente*, and the most peace-oriented of the American would-be presidential candidates at the time, Eugene McCarthy, made this naively clear, saying that the Czech invasion was not a real crisis. It was not, for the relationship between the United States and the Soviet Union.

There were of course several stretches of *détente* in the post-war period before the one which set in after 1962, and the memory of how rapidly the 1955 *détente* was destroyed in 1956 has naturally tended to make analysts wary of the later one. As I said, the *détente* is at best a kind of loose planking, which any ill-calculating manoeuvre can dislodge, temporarily at least. On the other hand, since it has this loose provisional quality, it can be put back together again fairly rapidly, and its temporary disturbance is not necessarily something that has to be avoided at all costs. A Western policy which made excessive concessions to avoid disturbing the *détente* would be unwarranted, since all the indications are that it is rather more necessary at present to the Soviet Union than to the West.

On the other hand, if *détente* ought not to be bought at too high a price, neither ought it to be feared as necessarily a Trojan horse. An interesting case-study here is the attitude of John Foster Dulles to the *détente* assiduously pressed upon the West by the Soviet decision-makers roughly from a year or so before Stalin's death in 1953 until the ' summit ' meeting of 1955. Dulles was intensely suspicious of it, apparently on the somewhat simplistic reasoning that anything the Soviet Union was promoting could not be good for the West, and that a spell of diplomatic fine weather would cause the NATO alliance to fall apart. But in fact *détente* then proved a good deal more dangerous and destructive to the Soviet system than to the Western one. It was a major cause of the weakening of the Sino-Soviet alliance, and of the ferment in Eastern Europe. Well before Stalin's death, in fact over the whole period from the bid for a Korean truce in early 1951 up to the Austrian treaty, there are clear indications that Soviet decision-makers felt themselves in a vulnerable situation (over-extended) and were therefore in a mood to liquidate doubtful ventures and redefine commitments, with a view to easing tensions with the West. They had good reason to want this, since some American policy-advisers during the just-preceding period had come to assume that general war might be only a fortnight away. The Soviet mood of orientation towards concessions has never since 1955 recurred over anything like so long a span of time as these four years (early '51 to mid'-55), and I think one can therefore still classify as the major missed opportunity of the postwar period the failure seriously to investigate Stalin's note of March 1952 concerning German unification. That was of course Adenauer's decision rather than Dulles's, but it illustrates an attitude which he shared with Dulles, and which the latter sustained when he became Secretary of State a few months later. Bidault once observed of Dulles that he talked a lot about calculated risks, when what he really meant was that he spent a lot of time calculating and risked nothing. This determination to play it safe, inducing suspicion of the *détente*, postponed the process of negotiation with the Russians until after the period in which they had felt themselves seriously vulnerable, and in which they had therefore been inclined to make concessions. That mood of Soviet policy has not recurred in European affairs, and relations with China are the only possibility one can see of its again being induced. The moral of the whole episode seems to be that if the adversary contrives a *détente*, as the Soviet Union undoubtedly did in this period, it may be because the politicians concerned need one, for internal or other reasons, rather than because they are far-sightedly digging traps for future use. Decision-makers are in fact usually too busy staving off immediate crises to have much time to plan for the next but three.

Of the four factors which I have called the bases of the present system of crisis management, it is only in the last that one can readily see much prospect of disruptive change. No defensive system is likely to be effective enough to end the exchange of hostages; surveillance systems appear in a fair way to grow towards absoluteness and towards symmetry as between the dominant powers (ultimately including China); the strategic ideology shared by the United States and the Soviet Union has already proved strong enough to sustain some measure of agreement at the Strategic Arms Limitation Talks. But as to the fourth element, the bias towards preponderant power on the side of the *status quo*, the Chinese would of course say that they are changing all that. So they may be, if one thinks on a Chinese time-scale, in which fifty years is a sort of eyelid-blink in history. But Westerners characteristically take short views, and for the fifteen years or so across which it seems feasible to attempt a forecast of the shape of world power distribution and the provenance of crisis, no sudden accretion of strength to the side of the revolution appears likely.

5

INSTRUMENTS AND TECHNIQUES OF CRISIS MANAGEMENT

EVERY crisis is an exceedingly complex set of interactions, a confluence of decisions some of whose sources are very difficult to trace. Each of the historical episodes which I intend to dispose of in a paragraph or two in this chapter would warrant examination at book-length, and some of them, for instance Cuba '62 and Suez '56, have already been the subject of several such studies. Here I shall be looking at them in shorthand outlines, so to speak, simply as illustrations of particular modes of handling crises which seem to me to have grown up in the postwar period. There are considerable similarities, as I have said before, between the contemporary conventions and those of earlier periods of crisis management, but these similarities have not often been recognized by the decision-makers or even the academic analysts of the process. Perhaps every generation feels obliged to re-invent its world, and to assume that its conventions are new.

The distinction between instruments on the one hand and techniques on the other in crisis management is not altogether easy to sustain, but I shall take the former word to indicate *what* is used, and the second *how* it is used. On this distinction, the basic instrument of crisis management is what I shall call the signal, and the techniques are mostly ways of using signals. By signal I mean a threat or offer communicated to the other party or parties to the crisis.

Such signals are not necessarily verbal messages. Some of the sharpest and most effective of them are movements of military resources of various sorts. For instance, when the Russians appointed the second-in-command to their most noted rocket expert as Commander-in-Chief of their Far Eastern military district at a time of sharp border clashes between themselves and China, the appointment was a more brusque signal about the possible nature of future hostilities there than words would have been.[1] Similarly, the Russian sending of Victor Louis, a ' journalist ' who does ill-defined diplomatic odd jobs for the

[1] General Tobulko, appointed in July 1969.

Russian government, to Taiwan[2] at a time when the Chinese were hinting at the possibility of a settlement with America, was probably a signal that the island might have another protector than the Seventh Fleet. This obviously is the sort of thing that it would be politically difficult to say in words, until the hinted shift of a relationship was an accomplished fact. The hint may prevent the actuality being necessary. Border hostilities themselves are a kind of signal: it is hard to make sense of Russian incursions over the Sinkiang border save as a signal to the Chinese of the vulnerability of their nuclear installations there. In fact, in the obscure border crises of March–October 1969 between China and Russia, one might interpret the whole of Russian policy as an exercise in crisis management by signal, i.e. by communicated threat. The means of communication were most elaborate and varied, including a Russian letter to Communist parties outside the Communist world, apparently constructed to be interpreted as a bid for support in the case of a Russian strike at China.

Signalling is as essential to crisis management as to a busy airport. But there is a good deal more scope for ambiguity in signalling in the diplomatic field than in that of transport. An ambiguous signal when driving may be a prelude to disaster, but in diplomacy ambiguity in signalling may be creative.

A good instance of this is what came to be known as the ' Trollope ploy ' in the Cuban missile crisis. The ' Trollope ploy ' has been defined as ' the acceptance of an offer that has not been made, in order to induce the adversary to accept the acceptance '. The name (apparently conferred by Robert Kennedy) derives from those many Victorian heroines in the novels of Anthony Trollope who interpret a squeeze of the hand on the hero's part as a proposal of marriage, and who are successful in making this interpretation stick. In the Cuban case the ambiguity of communication was Mr Khrushchev's: he sent two letters, one implying a hard line about the American blockade, the other a mild and even yielding one. To deepen the confusion, it was not clear whether the ' hawklike ' letter (which was received second) had been written before or after

[2] In Oct. 1968; see Hsinhua New Agency daily bulletin, 7 Mar. 1969. Later he made an equally surprising appearance in Israel.

the 'dovelike' one. The American policy decision (the Trollope ploy) was to treat the 'dovelike' letter as the true communication, more or less ignoring the other (though it was received second, was probably written second, and might normally have been interpreted as the Russians' final position). It was this creative use of ambiguity which enabled the settlement to be reached.[3]

It may be objected that this was an exceptional case, and that ambiguity is more usually a dangerous and potentially disastrous element in crisis signalling. Many eminent practitioners in the field have implied as much. Mr Dulles, for instance, maintained and perhaps believed that the Korean war had been precipitated by a misleading or ambiguous signal by Dean Acheson when he was Secretary of State: Acheson's definition of the US defence perimeter in Asia as running down the island chain from Japan through Okinawa to the Philippines. This, according to the Republican interpretation, was assumed in Moscow to mean that South Korea would not be defended by US troops, and so led to the Russian miscalculation of allowing the North Koreans to initiate their take-over bid for South Korea. It was, of course, a very partisan version of the events which produced the Korean war, but short of the production of the North Korean equivalent of Cabinet minutes for the period concerned, there is no way of actually disproving it. Mr Dulles, however, was himself uncommonly proud of a diplomatic success which must be held to have been gained largely by a conscious or unconscious use of ambiguity in diplomatic signalling. This was during the Quemoy-Matsu crisis of 1958, the management of which he sometimes described as his finest achievement. The ambiguity resided in the difference between the line apparently signalled by President Eisenhower's speeches during this crisis (mild, conciliatory, and seemingly ready to abandon the islands to the Chinese Communists) and the line signalled by Mr Dulles during the same period (tough, intransigent, and ready to back the Chinese Nationalists' determination to retain the islands by all means including atomic weapons). These conflicting signals were differentially received by the adversary alliance, China and the Soviet Union,

[3] See Robert Kennedy, *Thirteen Days* (1969).

which still at this time functioned as such, even though the Lebanon-Jordan crisis a few weeks earlier had made a large crack in it. The Russians 'selected' the tougher American signals, as transmitted by Mr Dulles as the true definition of the American posture. The Chinese 'selected' the milder line, as transmitted by the President, since it was more compatible with their overall view of the balance of forces in the world, and the Maoist propositions that the 'East Wind was prevailing over the West Wind' and that 'all imperialists are paper tigers'. Since it was the Russians who actually controlled the weaponry, their view of the situation prevailed, and the Chinese had to retreat to the ritualized expression of the conflict by shelling Quemoy and Matsu on alternate days. The Americans not only obtained their optimum objectives in the crisis area (retaining the islands without having to fight for them) but a very large bonus indeed in the fact that the Sino-Soviet alliance never recovered from this difference of interpretation. Within a year the partners had gone their separate ways: Mr Khrushchev symbolically on his journey to meet Eisenhower at Camp David, and the Chinese along the road to independent nuclear status. So Mr Dulles had some reason to count this among his prime successes, though I do not know that he ever conceded that ambiguity was among his techniques.

Such differential receipt of signals is easier to see as between members of an alliance, and one could cite instances of it in the case of NATO members, for example in the various Berlin crises, but the more interesting case is that of differential receipt (and transmission) of signals as between different elements in a single decision-making élite. In a sense all such élites, even in a totalitarian state, are coalitions or alliances of various interests, and ought always theoretically to be open to differential signalling. One can see this very easily if one looks at the British and German decision-making élites during the run-up to the Second World War, and thinks of the role of Dahlerus, the 'Cliveden set', the illusions of Hess, and so on. It is more surprising when one sees it in the case of a long-joined and apparently monolithic decision-making élite such as that of Maoist China. Yet if one looks at the accusations against Lo Jui-ching and others accused of 'taking the bourgeois military road ' during the Cultural Revolution in China, they are really based on the military professionals having interpreted differently the signals from American military action in Vietnam, and therefore wanting an approach to the Soviet Union in the hope of advanced weapons procurement. One must therefore say that ambiguity, based on differential signalling, is a possible technique *vis-à-vis* a single government even if totalitarian, as well as towards alliances.

There are, however, more straightforward instruments that must seem entitled to claim a role in crisis management: law, economic pressures, intermediaries, arbitration and conciliation procedures, international institutions. One would not deny that all these are potentially useful, yet examining the crises of the postwar period one would not say that they have been very conspicuously used and successful. Concepts of what is internationally legal no doubt influence the choices made by decision-makers in crisis situations, but on the evidence the influences have been rather marginal. Economic pressures have been used: for instance, the threat of oil sanctions in the Suez crisis was part of the combination of factors which modified British policy. But when used alone, as in the Rhodesia case, they do not seem decisive. Intermediaries of various sorts have had their successes (and rather more often their failures). The ability of the UN to provide inspection teams, peace-keeping forces, truce commissions, and the like has been an essential element in the success of what may be called the ' tidying-up ' phase of many a crisis. Yet when the UN role is examined more closely in particular crisis situations, it will be seen very often to consist of conferring legitimacy on crisis management by the great powers, and the same is true of the roles of other organizations such as NATO, or the OAS.

Most importantly, we must look at the question of the choice of particular kinds of weapons systems, and military structures, as an influence on crisis management. This is a very large subject, and full of uncertainties. Theoretically, the choice of weapons systems ought to be one of the most useful modes of controlling crises, but the ' lead time ' for modern weapons systems is five to ten years, or even longer in some categories, and predicting what the crises of ten years hence are going to look like, and what forces-in-being will be most useful for reducing their dangers is thus a somewhat difficult project.

One can of course point to the obvious desirability of built-in devices against the unauthorized or accidental tripping of retaliation systems in times of crisis, such as the ' permissive action ' link, the ' fail-safe ' system, and various ' two keys ' sets of arrangements. Luckily this is a field in which the interests of the two dominant powers are so nearly identical that a surprising amount of information has been deliberately passed. President Kennedy was the decision-maker on this. Just after his inauguration there was a near-disaster of a nuclear kind, when a bomber on a training flight with two 24-megaton bombs crashed in North Carolina. The bombs had six inter-locking safety devices, but on one of them five of these devices had been triggered by the crash, so that only one switch prevented a detonation. This incident, and the information that there had been about sixty near-accidents since the end of the Second World War, including the launching of two actual missiles with nuclear warheads, alarmed Kennedy into the consciousness that it was desirable not only that the US should improve its accident-proofing, but that the Russians should have equally good techniques in this field, and should know what the American systems were. He therefore authorized a Pentagon man, John McNaughton, to provide a good deal of information on these devices at an Arms Control symposium in December 1962, and via US scientists to Russian scientists at a Pugwash conference.[4] The Russians are now known to have developed similar accident-proofing devices. One hopes that in due course information of these techniques also reached the Chinese, and has been used.

Even this kind of precaution is not without its ambivalences. Better accident-proofing means that missiles are more readily put on ' full alert ' and this has some uncertain side effects on crisis decision making.

As yet it is difficult to say much about the influence of the most advanced prospective weapons systems on crisis manage-

[4] This incident has not, as far as I know, been officially acknowledged but there was some leakage to the press about it, see *Newsweek*, 5 May 1969.

ment. In the early days of the ABM debate it was assumed by many analysts that the deployment of ABMs would dangerously undermine the *détente*, and since the *détente* is both a product of, and a necessity for, sound crisis management, this would of course be a most damaging turn of events. But in fact the ABM debate and the beginnings of deployment have now extended over about eight years, and there is little or no sign of the *détente* being adversely affected. On the contrary, it might be argued that an agreed and symmetrical deployment of ' thin ' ABM systems in both Russia and America is likely further to strengthen the *détente*. The argument against the ABM was roughly to the effect that the *détente* rested on the ability of Russia and America to inflict ' unacceptable levels of damage ' on each other, and that therefore it might be undermined by reducing those unacceptable levels of damage, or in more technical terms, that its ' damage-limiting ' capacity was destabilizing. ABMs may have other undesirable qualities and side effects (such as being very expensive and producing some fallout dangers to the populations of the cities concerned) but they have not undermined the *détente* in that particular way. There has been in fact a good deal of inconsistency in the anti-ABM argument, in that the opponents of the system have argued both that it will be relatively ineffective (which is probably true for the moment but might change on the basis of techniques now emerging) and that it must have a damaging effect on the *détente* (which would imply that it would be relatively effective, having more ' damage-limiting ' capacity than has as yet developed). Arguments about the ill effects on the *détente* are arguments about probable Russian psychological reactions to the system, and they seem to have been falsified by actual Russian statements and behaviour. The Russians, with their usual defensive-mindedness, have simply seen this as a shield of sorts for their cities, and have determined to have it on that basis, without bothering about the elaborate American calculations concerning the stability of the overall balance. They may possibly want it *vis-à-vis* China and other powers, even if its effectiveness against the US remains low.

The development of MIRVs is in a different category. Some policy-makers have implied that they might restore the prospect of either side again regarding a first-strike capacity—i.e. a capacity for decisive surprise attack—as possible. This would indeed be a disastrous development, since it would mean in any crisis that the chief decision-makers on either side would hear some voices urging pre-emptive strike. In such conditions, a nuclear Armageddon would become a great deal more likely. But the argument that either side will believe that it can attain a first-strike capacity is unconvincing, unless it can be shown that the second-strike capacity of Polaris and its successors and their Russian equivalents can be effectively counteracted by ABMs and other means. There does not seem much sign of this.

Nor should it be assumed that even if, by some major miracle, the whole apparatus of *avant-garde* warfare were abolished, and the knowledge of how to reconstruct it were wiped from men's minds, and their libraries, the peace would be saved and sober crisis management assured. In 1914 all it took for the structure of the armed forces to have a profoundly disastrous effect on the management of that crisis was an old contingency plan and some railway timetables.

Having said so much about these instruments and techniques, we have now to look a little at how they have worked out in some of the crises of the postwar period, both adversary and intramural. Analysis of the predominant unresolved crises of the time of writing, in Indo-China and the Middle East, has been reserved to the final chapter.

Let us start by considering the Suez crisis, because it lay more or less on the border between the two categories, adversary and intramural, and to my mind shows that the management of a crisis may determine its very nature.[5] Oddly enough, the outcome in this case seems to have depended partly on the insistence of some members of the State Department on playing up, in fact exaggerating, its alleged dangers as a potential adversary crisis. Robert Murphy, who was by no means sympathetic to this point of view, quotes some of his colleagues as wailing that they might be ' burned to a crisp ',[6] meaning presumably that they took seriously the heavy Soviet hints of military action

---

[5] Rather on the analogy of the infant bee, which, if fed on royal jelly, will become a queen bee, but if sustained on more prosaic stuff will become a worker.

[6] *Diplomat among Warriors*, p. 476.

(rockets) on behalf of the Egyptians. The Foreign Office entirely discounted this threat, and was I think right to do so. What we know of the weakness of Soviet missile forces even six years later, in 1962, plus the caution with which the Soviet Union has always avoided any military involvement with the Arabs in their encounters with Israel (other of course than the supply of arms and instructors) inclines one to feel even more convinced now than at the time that there was never any real possibility of a military initiative by Russia in reaction to the British and French collusion with Israel. Nevertheless the Russian threat, empty though it was, provided a considerable part of the rationale for the arm-twisting American technique of managing this episode as an intramural crisis of the Anglo-American alliance. (The French simply acquiesced, somewhat resentfully, in the British decisions. It was also of course an intramural crisis of the American-Israeli tacit alliance, managed by similar methods though separate measures.) In the British case, the effective arm-twisting was undoubtedly economic: the threat of oil sanctions and the necessity of stopping the run on the pound.[7] Britain is peculiarly vulnerable to this kind of technique, and so in a slightly different way is Israel. But the number of other countries of which this is true is surprisingly small, and on the whole economic sanctions have shown themselves relatively ineffective as a mode of management of either adversary or intramural crisis, a point which later became painfully obvious to British policy-makers in connection with Rhodesia.

I said that this was successfully managed as an intramural crisis of the Anglo-American alliance, and I think in terms of my three criteria for success this was fairly clearly the case, as far as Britain was concerned, though one might put up the contrary argument as far as the Franco-American alliance was concerned. At least in the British case, the alliance was no less effective from 1957 than before it: in many ways closer than ever, in fact, on matters such as nuclear weapons.[8] The British

---

[7] For an examination specifically of the Anglo-American relationship in the Suez crisis see Richard E. Neustadt, *Alliance Politics* (New York, 1970).

[8] This question is treated in more detail in the author's *The Debatable Alliance* (London, 1964).

were not permanently shaken in their attachment to the alliance: the credibility or credit of the US as an ally was not diminished. But one might, as I said, give different answers on all these criteria with regard to France, and I think one must concede that the Anglo-American situation is rather exceptional among alliances in that the sense of an overriding common interest is or has been so strong as to sustain, without undue fraying, some exceedingly sharp clashes of specific interests in particular areas. One cannot generalize from this particular alliance-relationship to others: the French attitude is nearer the norm.

The Congo crisis of 1960–1 is a second instance of the fact that managing a crisis intramurally may be one technique of averting its more dangerous development as an adversary crisis. In the initial phase of events in the Congo, during the first breakdown of coherent government in 1960, there seem to have been real possibilities of its turning into quite a danger-ous confrontation between the United States and the Soviet Union. I would regard Mr Khrushchev's policies in the early phase of this crisis as showing the same adventurist tendency to leap at opportunities for the quick spectacular success abroad that he showed in 1962 in the Cuban missile crisis. The original Soviet bid for expansion of influence in a Congo run by Lumumba was defeated chiefly by Mr Andrew Cordier's action in closing the airfields. He was then operating as an official of the UN and perhaps we can regard it as a happy coincidence that the UN official concerned happened to be an American citizen, and a former member of the State Department, with a very adequate understanding of the national interest. How-ever, in the later phase of the crisis, after Lumumba's death, the Soviet Union might very well have reasserted its efforts to make diplomatic gains in the Congo, by for instance a more whole-hearted backing of the remaining Lumumbaists. The fact that by and large the Russians did not really work hard at such a project must I think be put down in part to the quite tough-minded American management of the intramural crisis with its NATO allies and their friends, in this case Belgium, Katanga, Britain, and Rhodesia. It seems fair to assume that the US determination to back the UN's rather extravagant notions of its own powers and capabilities was a factor which in part

' bought off ' the Soviet Union, and in part reduced the Russian leverage. Thus the intramural crisis was the price paid for averting an adversary crisis.

Whether this success was worth all the incidental costs is another question. In this case I do not mean costs in terms of the NATO alliance, but costs in terms of the intermediary [9] in the crisis: the UN. The then Secretary-General, Dag Hammarskjoeld, brooding in his mystical Swedish way over the emergence of sovereign African states into world politics, seems to have believed that the UN would be a central factor in African political evolution (and in crisis management there) over the succeeding decades. But in fact the UN has exerted very little real or effective influence in the endemic African crises since the Congo, and one might argue that this was because the UN over-extended itself in every sense in this first crisis, especially financially and in the resources of intellect and energy expended by the Secretariat. There is a macabrely appropriate symbol of this in the fact that it cost Hammarskjoeld his own life.

Every crisis raises the question of whether there is any function for an intermediary, and who will be the one most likely to be useful. And in every case many voices will suggest that it should be the UN, probably the Secretary-General. This is, so to speak, a convenient shelf onto which any awkward diplomatic package tends to be shoved. But it is by no means true that every crisis benefits by the services of an intermediary, or that the Secretary-General or any other official of the UN is necessarily the right intermediary if one is required. And it is furthermore always necessary to offset the real costs to the intermediary institution (in terms of its later usefulness) against the advantages of its use in the particular crisis concerned. Counting up all the costs to the UN of its intermediary role in this case (including Hammarskjoeld's death, and all that stemmed from it), I am not entirely sure that the sum comes out positive.

---

[9] There are to my mind two kinds of possible middlemen in a crisis: I shall call them intermediaries and interveners. The distinction is that the intermediary's power stems purely from the will of the principals: the intervener has some independent base of power to interfere, whether the parties consent or not.

There is one mode of adversary crisis which offers no scope for being turned into an intramural crisis (though it may have intramural repercussions on either or both sides) and that is the direct head-on collision of interests between two dominant powers: America and Russia, America and China, China and Russia. I shall take the Cuban '62 crisis as the model for the first of these. There is indeed a prevalent tendency to take it as a model for all crises, largely I think because it had such an attractive cast of characters. But this tendency should be resisted, because Cuba as a model for crises generally is misleading in the same way as a child's model of a farm is misleading for farms generally: it is neater, brighter, more *determinate* than life. Most crises tend to have a more sprawling, formless, unsatisfactory, repetitious shape.

However, if the crisis itself is not a universally applicable model, the behaviour of the chief decision-maker and his advisers on the Western side still seems to me to be so, informed by great moral and intellectual sensitivity, perception, imagination, and courage. The mode of resolution of the adversary crisis is so well known that there seems no need for further analysis. The factors in the American success were, first, local superiority in conventional forces (in this case, naval) which meant that the adversary decision-maker, if he wanted to raise his stakes, had to raise them to the level of nuclear encounter; secondly, the overall strategic superiority, which in fact inhibited him from doing that; and third, the skill and judgement with which the President and his advisers built bridges behind the adversary to facilitate his retreat.

There are some aspects of the crisis which are less well understood, and may therefore warrant more examination. It was, one might say, the first crisis of the age of surveillance. That is to say, the form that the crisis took, and the moment of its precipitation, were determined by intelligence gathering in the modern manner, i.e. the discovery of the missile sites by U-2 overflights. The instrument of surveillance has since become the satellite-mounted television camera rather than the U-2, and this is a more extreme form of a growing class distinction between America and Russia on the one hand, and their respective allies on the other. The US, and the USSR, with a vastly greater knowledge of the technology in this field (one of the fringe benefits from the space race), must increasingly be confronted by the problem of how much of the information so gathered to communicate to allies, and at what stage, and how to convince them that the information is reliable, means what it is taken to mean, and warrants the action proposed. In such episodes there must be tension between on the one hand the desire to have military plans completed before disclosure, even to allied decision-makers under pledges of secrecy, and on the other hand the necessity of carrying those allies and public opinion with the chief decision-maker. (The impact of public opinion on crisis management will be considered in more detail later.) Clearly President Kennedy took great trouble in this instance, by the despatch of Dean Acheson and others to Europe, to ensure that the information turned up by the CIA carried suitable diplomatic weight. But it can hardly be said that he consulted his NATO allies in the crisis management (though one could regard the informal role of the British Ambassador in the policy-making process as akin to such consultation with Britain, the Ambassador acting as a proxy for the Prime Minister, if not the government, by a process of telephone communication). One can argue that a greater appearance of consultation would have prevented such intra-mural repercussions from the crisis as did develop within NATO. But I would be inclined to make the contrary argument. When a crisis blows up so fast the other members of the alliance are somewhat in the situation of passengers in a car going into a skid: it is not necessarily advantageous for them to have time to develop lines of advice to the chief decision-maker. Nor is it true that a known or assumed process of crisis decision-sharing on an allied basis would necessarily conduce to the safer management of crises. The crucial element is the expectations of the adversary decision-makers, and their ability to predict reactions correctly. Anything which complicates this calculation for them (such as having to allow for the influence of allies) probably increases the risk of error, and thus the chance of disaster. In the Cuban case this risk was largely removed by the known existence of an arbitrary time limit for decision, imposed by the length of time known to be necessary for the completion of the missile installations. Since the time span was very short, the prospect of real consultation, and real allied influence on the Washington decision-making, was ruled out *and was known to the Russians to be ruled out*. So their calculations had to encompass only American attitudes and, luckily, they got the answer right.

Nothing fails like failure, as the saying goes, and so the intramural (and perhaps domestic) repercussions of the Cuban crisis were much greater on the Soviet side of the balance than on the American side. The most important of these repercussions were with China rather than Cuba—Dr Castro was indignant enough, but was mollified by lavish financial aid.[10] For China, however, Mr Khrushchev's management of the crisis provided reasonably substantial grounds for Chinese accusations of both ' adventurism ' (for putting the missiles in) and ' capitulationism ' (for taking them out). All in all, it was certainly the largest and most effective item in the Chinese case against general Russian strategy in the long-drawn-out struggle of ' peaceful coexistence ' with the capitalist world.

The recurrent Berlin crises offer a clear contrast to Cuba in respect of the possibilities of consultation, and the development of some kind of allied crisis management, even though with an overriding vote for the United States. The primary reason for this distinction is the difference in military responsibilities and potentialities in the two areas. In the Caribbean the United States neither wants nor expects military help from its European allies, and the whole tenor of American foreign policy tradition since the Monroe Doctrine has been to look with suspicion and resentment on any European claim for a voice or influence in the Latin American area. Of all the areas of potential crisis, it is perhaps the one in which allied management or serious consultation with the Europeans is least likely. Would it be too harsh to say that consultation with Latin American states is also rather a formality? It is somewhat difficult to believe that American policy on Cuba or the Dominican Republic or

[10] Which has since continued at a rate equivalent to about $300m. a year. The Americans are quite contented about this, reasoning apparently that this continuing illustration of the costs of gathering allies will damp Russian enthusiasm for more such ventures.

Guatemala would have been changed if the government of Argentina or Brazil or Mexico had raised an objection to the proposed action. The diplomatic support of Latin American countries is useful to the United States, but their military co-operation is not necessary, and in moments of crisis distant prospects of diplomatic resentment are not likely to be a major preoccupation.

The Berlin situation illustrates the opposite case: the military co-operation as well as the diplomatic support of America's major NATO allies is necessary if reaction to any kind of challenge is to look credible. Therefore it is a quite exceptional candidate for allied crisis management. Possibly the history of the city also helps in this respect. There is a general recognition that Berlin has been an area of latent crisis over the whole period since 1948, or even 1945, and thus by the time of the most recent dangerous-looking rise in tension, that of 1958–61, joint contingency planning was a long-standing routine. This was not necessarily an unmixed blessing: familiarity with a problem seems sometimes to result in the overlooking of some of the options available to the adversary. That the Russians might build a wall actually across the city was not one of the contingencies for which plans were prepared (though walls elsewhere had been thought of) and so Western policy was in fact rather hesitant in the first week or so of the Russian operation.

However, one can see the building of the wall as part of the resolution phase of the Berlin crisis, rather than its development phase. In fact, there is a certain hopefulness in the history of Berlin as a *locale* for crisis since 1948. If it illustrates the reality of the conflict between the Western powers and the Soviet Union, it also illustrates the resourcefulness both sides have devoted to preventing this conflict from flaring into actual hostilities over a period of more than twenty years. And in that span of time, one might argue, Berlin has been turned from a true *source* of crisis, to a *symbol* of crisis, where tension is consciously turned on and off as a gesture or a signal. This was, I think, the true quality of the subcrisis of 1969.

In fact, I would argue that for many crisis points the only available technique of management may be 'ritualized hostilities '. That is, where one of the parties is not willing to abandon its claim, yet not able to make it effective (or at least not prepared to take the risks incidental to doing so), it may opt for the *ritual* of pressure as a substitute for its actuality. It would be too optimistic to argue that Berlin is as yet firmly in this category, but I think we may say that both Panmunjon and Quemoy-Matsu present situations of ritualized hostilities. At Panmunjon where the Korean armistice has never been turned into a peace, the ritual has been maintained now for more than fifteen years with the regular diplomatic meetings for denunciation of the other side; as a final macabre touch it has even become a tourist attraction. Busloads of visitors are taken to see the confrontation. The Quemoy-Matsu ritual was more directly military: the islands were shelled regularly on alternate days. Possibly there is something in Far Eastern cultures which makes ritual as a substitute for reality more acceptable than it usually has been in the West. The most extreme case of this was the final mechanism for resolving the *Pueblo* crisis; the handing-over of the American captives in return for an American apology *which had been publicly and officially disavowed in advance by the American authorities*.

In its earlier stages, however, the *Pueblo* crisis was subjected to a technique which I am inclined to call ' load shedding '. If it had occurred in a period of reasonable calm, the seizure of an American intelligence ship and its crew by North Korean forces when it was either just inside or just outside North Korean waters might have provoked a very sharp reaction from the American government.[11] American public opinion was certainly much incensed. But it occurred at a time when the decision-making machinery in Washington was already overloaded in consequence of the Tet offensive of 1968 in Vietnam. And just as a sophisticated electrical system is programmed to shed part of the load when the total load rises above a certain point, so in this case a similar process of load shedding seems to have taken place. It may have been partly accidental rather than built purposely into the system; for instance it took

[11] The US Navy still claims that the ship was never inside the twelve-mile limit: the North Koreans say it was apprehended about nine miles out. Obviously no watertight case can now ever be made for either claim.

forty minutes, after the *Pueblo's* plight was known, for the US Navy officials in Japan to reach Air Force headquarters by telephone, and the Air Force in any case did not have planes ready in South Korea for quick reaction, and those in Okinawa could not reach the *Pueblo* in time.[12] However, the fortuitous circumstance that the US armed forces were not able to react immediately did not of course rule out the possibility of later reaction by Washington against North Korea: in an earlier epoch some form of reprisal raid would have been mounted or at least threatened against the Korean port in which the *Pueblo* was held. But in fact the Washington decision-making machinery seems simply to have shed this extra load, imposed at a time when it was already under heavy strain. This possibility is an inevitable side effect of the speed of modern communications. Because Washington can normally be swiftly consulted in crisis (and because the risks are so heavy) the tendency is always to refer back, rather than take a local initiative. And rightly: as President Kennedy once said, the alternative danger is some sergeant starting World War III. Yet this system means that the central decision-making machinery must be at times overloaded, and must therefore have some built-in ability to shed loads.

There are resemblances between this 'load-shedding' reaction to crisis and the more organized technique used in Laos, which I would be inclined to call 'putting it on the back burner'. The Laos crisis, occasioned by the breakdown of the 1954 agreements, was the first which confronted President Kennedy when he came into office in January 1961. Decisions involving the possible commitment of US troops were demanded, even earlier than those demanded on the disastrous Cuban invasion project. Moreover, there were wide differences of opinion within the American government (particularly between the CIA, Defense, and State); and competing pulls on American policy from three allies, the Thais wanting stronger American backing for the right-wing generals, and the British and French urging support for the neutralist Prince, Souvanna Phouma.

In this situation Kennedy's policy was, it might be said, in

[12] USA House Repres, Special Subcommittee, Inquiry into the USS *Pueblo* and EC-121 plane incidents: *Report;* 91st Congress, 1st sess., 28 July 1969.

the best nineteenth-century tradition: he consulted the ruler of the adversary dominant power, Mr Khrushchev (at Vienna in April 1961), agreed with him on a conference, and accepted the conference ' solution ' of tripartite government. In fact this arrangement (embodied in the Geneva Agreements of 1962) did not in any way *solve* the problems of Laos from the point of view of Western policy-makers. It did not secure a genuine neutrality for Laos, or reduce the use of the Ho Chi Minh trail through the country by North Vietnamese supplies, or provide domestic stability, or end the in-fighting within Laos to control the government, or reduce the ability of the Pathet Lao to hold their area of military control. The whole process simply established an accommodation between the dominant powers: an agreement that the situation in Laos should be set aside while the real battle was fought out in Vietnam. That is, it was tacitly agreed that the Laos situation should stay ' on the back burner ' until some resolution was approached in Vietnam. In 1970–1 Laos (and Cambodia) came ' off the back burner ' as a consequence of a new turn to the war in Vietnam. But since the fate of Laos was bound in any case to be determined by what happened in Vietnam, a mode of avoiding a second front there was convenient for both the main parties involved, and gave the Laotians some years' respite from the worst effects of a full military encounter.

Let us now turn to look at a few instances of intramural crisis, and particularly at the way in which these crises affect relations between the dominant power and its allies. The minor members of an alliance system trade full independence of action for (among other things) protection and influence on the policy of the dominant power concerned. Sometimes, as in the case of NATO, they make the bargain willingly, convinced at least at the time of signature of the alliance that the benefits outweigh the costs and risks. Sometimes, as in the case of the Warsaw Pact, they face a forced or ambiguous choice. But in either case the dominant power within the alliance is the major factor in deciding not only how the alliance will stand in adversary crises, but in what spirit and with what degree of consultation the intramural crises of the alliance will be managed.

It is obviously difficult to find much evidence as to how far the Soviet Union has consulted other members of the Warsaw Pact on its management of the main intramural crises of its alliance systems (Yugoslavia 1948, East Germany 1953, Hungary and Poland 1956, China 1959–62, Czechoslovakia and Rumania 1968–9, Poland again 1970). About all one can say is that there does appear some indication that during the later of these episodes the Soviet Union was anxious to have the diplomatic support (and the equal military involvement, if necessary) of other members of the Pact, and that it may thus have been influenced in the decision to invade Czechoslovakia by Poland and East Germany. In the crisis with China in 1968–9, which must as I said earlier be classed as adversary rather than intramural, the Soviet policy-makers were obviously concerned to have East European support. Perhaps one ought to conclude that there is evolving some trend in the Soviet sphere towards allied crisis management, a reluctant concession on the part of the Russian decision-makers, and that this may give the East Europeans some measure of diplomatic leverage against the Soviet Union.

However, most observations of how the process of intramural crisis management works are necessarily drawn from the various alliance systems in which the United States is the dominant power, since these are so much more open to inspection. I shall largely confine my examination to the process within NATO, because this is the most interesting and complex (though not the most typical) case, and because it provides the widest spectrum of crises. The reason why I do not regard the NATO system as really typical is because the other members of NATO have an unusually equal relation, in military potential and diplomatic skill, with the United States. Two of them, for instance, are nuclear powers (Britain and France) and another, Germany, is a conventional military power of a major sort. All of them have long diplomatic experience. None of these factors exist in most American alliance relationships: the more usual situation is probably one like ANZUS, with the United States allied to one or two powers of small military strength and no great diplomatic leverage or experience.

Though all the American alliance systems have no doubt had their crises, those of NATO have had the most explosive potential, since NATO is the most important single alliance-mechanism affecting the central balance of power. The simplest and most obvious form of intramural crisis for NATO has perhaps been that presented by Cyprus:[13] a direct clash of wills and interests between two of the alliance members, Greece and Turkey, over a piece of territory of great ethnic importance to the one, and of strategic and emotional importance to the other. A third NATO power, Britain, is involved by reason of historic connection and its remaining bases on the island. The crises over Cyprus have undoubtedly at times damaged the functioning of the NATO alliance in the Eastern Mediterranean, and have threatened to damage it further by the possible exit of either Greece or Turkey. This however has been a theoretical rather than a real possibility, since neither the Greek nor the Turkish government, in a situation of growing Soviet naval strength in the Eastern Mediterranean, is at all likely to see any feasible alternative to NATO as a solution to its own security problems. The diplomatic leverage of each *vis-à-vis* the United States or NATO itself has therefore been quite restricted. Neither can in fact afford even to damage NATO severely, much less to leave it. And they have been inhibited, to a considerable degree, from using military force against each other on the island by pressures within NATO as well as from the United Nations. In effect, the crisis-management machinery of NATO (including the use of United Nations forces) has replaced the old imperial presence of Britain, restraining the conflict by setting the rules for the two chief parties in direct contact, the Greek and Turkish Cypriots on the island itself.

On the whole, though perhaps more by luck than judgement, the Cyprus crisis management seems to meet the three criteria I have suggested for the successful handling of intramural crisis. The functioning of the alliance has been somewhat damaged, but not to a crippling degree. The Greeks and the Turks may not be satisfied with their position in the alliance, or what it has done for them in this matter, but there is not much they can do about it. And the credit or credibility of the

---

[13] For a fuller account of the Cyprus crisis see, for instance, Robert Stephens, *Cyprus: a Place of Arms* (1966).

dominant member of the alliance, the United States, has not been damaged. It might even have been enhanced, at least with members other than Greece and Turkey, by the fact that the American emissaries who have at various times been interveners in the crisis—Dean Acheson, George Ball, Cyrus Vance[14] have done rather better by it than most others. If people assume these mediators have failed, it is because they do not distinguish adequately between crisis management and conflict resolution. They expect the crisis management to ' solve ' the Cyprus situation in some magical fashion that will end the conflict between the Greek and Turkish communities on the island, or between the sovereign states of Greece and Turkey. But these conflicts have very long historical roots, and are expressions of the tribal feelings of the two ethnic groups concerned. No diplomatic formula is going to make them disappear: they have to be lived with. Cyprus is therefore a prime instance of the persistence of a conflict along with the management of the crises to which that conflict gives rise.

There are various other points of interest that the management of the Cyprus crisis raises, including the role of the United Nations in this field (in which it is a frequently useful but always very expensive instrument) and the distinction between interveners and intermediaries. But one of the most notable points is frequently overlooked: its illustration of the limits of local decision-makers' ability nowadays to turn intramural crises into adversary crises of the central balance. I am not necessarily implying that the actual Greek or the Turkish decision-makers would have *wished* to do this: it would have been almost inconceivably irrational even for the most dedicated xenophobe. But a good deal of the local nationalist journalistic comment was of the order of ' this could be the occasion for World War III '. Such a claim was always exceedingly wide of the mark, and the reasons are of interest for their applicability elsewhere. The only probable occasions for World War III are those in which two or more of the dominant powers believe that they have major interests at

[14] See Philip Windsor, *Nato and the Cyprus Crisis* (London, Inst. for Strategic Studies, Adelphi papers, no. 14, 1964) for the earlier phase of the conflict.

stake. The areas and issues about which they are likely to make this assumption are few, and probably growing fewer. Cyprus has not so far been among them. The ability of minor—or even major—allies of the dominant powers to induce them to raise their stakes to this level is now almost non-existent, and this is reassuring, since it reduces the potential occasions for major war.

Looking at some intramural crises which have involved America's most important allies—Britain, France, West Germany, and Japan—one can see how limited is the leverage even of this vital group when it is opposed by a firmly held notion of the national interest of the dominant power. The Skybolt crisis is one of the most interesting of those affecting Anglo-American relations, because it involves a factor I am inclined to call ' expert's warp ', which I think has probably helped precipitate several other crises. By ' expert's warp ' I mean the tendency to reject the obvious and reasonable interpretation of the other party's intentions in favour of something more subtle. Even politicians quite often mean what they say. In this case the decision-maker concerned was Mr McNamara, who had been indicating for some time before the Nassau meeting of Kennedy and Macmillan that he was sceptical about Skybolt, the missile system with which the British government hoped to give the V bombers five years or so of extra life. The British policy-makers seem not to have taken this seriously, possibly because they knew the strength of the American air lobby determined on securing Skybolt's retention. However, McNamara won his point, as he had done in a number of similar domestic battles. No doubt Macmillan found a posture of astonished horror at the cancellation (and an implication that he would be fighting for his own political life unless some alternative weapons system were secured) a useful technique in obtaining Polaris instead. Undoubtedly Polaris was a more viable long-term delivery system for British nuclear capacity.

The only factor that inhibits one from putting this down as a crisis rather gracefully and adroitly managed by Macmillan to Britain's long-term advantage is the unlooked-for side effect on President de Gaulle: his use of the Polaris decision as a reason (or at any rate a rationalization) for the veto on British entry to the EEC. However, though for Britain the Skybolt crisis would have been satisfactorily resolved by the acquisition of Polaris, had it not been for this French complication, the origin of the crisis was in an asymmetry of national interest, or assumed national interest, between Britain and America. That is, the British originally assumed that it was important for them to prolong the life of the V bombers until the early 1970s, but their leverage, even added to that of the Air Force lobby in America, was not enough to turn McNamara from his cost-effectiveness conclusions. If the ultimate side effect of the alternative solution, British exclusion from EEC for the next ten years, had been understood, would the decision have been different? I am putting the question in this unfair form to illuminate a rather obscure point concerning the clash of national interests between allies. Even the prospect of very serious diplomatic damage to an important ally (i.e. British prospects of entry to the EEC) may not necessarily modify a decision taken on the basis of the assumed national interest of the dominant power.

Though it may be stretching the terminology, I would be inclined to classify the growth from 1958 of French dissatisfaction with its situation in NATO, as a slow-motion or cumulative crisis. The reason I hesitate about this usage is that there do seem advantages in limiting the term crisis to periods of fairly short duration: thirteen days in the case of Cuba, six months in the case of Suez. Yet the Congo presents a case in which it is difficult to avoid the conclusion that the crisis period stretched over about two years, and the recurring Cyprus and Berlin crises have also tended to be fairly lengthy. And on my criterion of the level of conflict within a relationship increasing to a degree that threatens to transform that relationship, one must judge that this has been a slow and cumulative process in the case of France in the alliance.

As in the case of Skybolt, we may say that the cause of the crisis was asymmetry of assumed national interest. The French had assumed (perhaps on the basis of de Gaulle's emotional nationalism, rather than any real strategic calculation) that the French national interest (or pride) required the transformation of NATO into a three-power directorate. This was the proposition advanced in de Gaulle's letter to Eisenhower in 1958. The American policy-makers assumed then, and went on assuming, that any modification of NATO in the direction required by the General would be damaging to the American national interest in good relations with its other NATO partners. Undoubtedly there was some failure of crisis management in the rather casual brush-off given to the initial letter: the American policy-makers seem not to have interpreted it as signalling a serious French determination to challenge the existing structure of the Western alliance. But it was, and the challenge was pressed (until the General's departure) as hard as French policy-makers could afford to go, without really exacting much in the way of concessions in Washington. Again one might say the evidence indicates that the leverage which even an important ally can exert on the American definition of what the American national interest requires in particular circumstances was not very notable.

If we look, for contrast, at the cases of Germany and Japan, we might incline to the view that in some ways a very vulnerable ally may be better able to exert leverage than a reasonably strong one. ' I may collapse under the strain ' is a useful threat, but only when it is credible. Thus it is certainly easier to use for, say, Thailand (so long as a non-collapsible Thailand is deemed necessary to US interests) than for Britain or France. Germany and Japan are in a different category: essentially very strong powers but with an assumed political vulnerability.

The history of the MLF project is a good example of the effect this assumption may have on policy. There is a category of illnesses called iatrogenic: those induced by the physician in the course of treating the patient for an assumed illness. On this analogy I would be inclined to regard the MLF as the occasion of an iatrogenic crisis (or, to be more accurate, subcrisis) induced by a set of diplomatic physicians in the State Department, benevolently intent on forestalling German policymakers' interest in their own nuclear weapons. The intended solution almost managed to create not only the problem it aimed to resolve, but a different and more intractable one: an adversary crisis with the Russians over the prospect of a German finger anywhere near the nuclear trigger. Fortunately, however, the MLF sank under the weight of doubts and counter-proposals, mostly British.[15]

Even while thinking this a deliverance, one can still regard the project as testimony to American policy-makers' wish to obviate in advance an ally's resentment at a situation of disadvantage and vulnerability. Against the solid reality of the differences of national interest between the United States and Germany, those between the United States and France, or the United States and Britain are marginal. Both Britain and France can live with the *status quo* in Europe without much travail of spirit, whereas for Germany the consciousness that the present and prospective *modus vivendi* with the Soviet Union is based on its own partition must always be a thorn in the mind. None of the most likely American strategies in Europe is wholly compatible with German interests: ' flexible response ' would make the country a battlefield, disengagement and reliance on the nuclear stalemate might tempt the Russians to adventures, cultivation of the *détente* may imply acceptance of the partition. The Czech invasion showed that the Russians could with impunity impose sharp limits on the *Ostpolitik*. Germany has been in a tight box diplomatically speaking, and thus there was undoubtedly a case for the leader of the alliance to exert some extra effort to ensure that the box looked as comfortable and spacious as possible. With the accession to office of Willy Brandt, German policy-making *vis-à-vis* the Soviet Union and Eastern Europe has moved into a phase whose problems (and crises, if any) seem likely to be of a different sort. It is misleading to think of it as a new Rapallo phase: even if it proves not totally dissimilar in some of its economic consequences, there does not at present appear any scope for the same sort of political consequences, yet it seems to mark a stage in the adoption of a more independent stance by Germany in the management of its own relations with the Soviet Union, though also the resignation of some national ambitions for West Germans.

Looking back over the history of these postwar crises as a whole, one is struck by a sense of how often the decision-

<hr />

[15] See Alastair Buchan, *The Multilateral Force: an Historical Perspective* (London, Inst. for Strategic Studies, Adelphi papers, no. 13, 1964).

makers seem to have been ' playing it off the cuff '; acting on the promptings of intuition or temperament rather than plan or logic. This is true even of someone like Adenauer: his long tenacious defence of the German national interest, as he saw it, *vis-à-vis* the Soviet Union probably had as much of improvisation as Willy Brandt's now has in different circumstances. The policy-maker is under some kind of pressure (usually domestic) to make a gesture: the gesture becomes a signal: if the signal seems to have succeeded in the sense of making a little space for manoeuvre, the policy is made to match the signal. One can see this in a number of instances. Consider Forrestal sending the USS *Missouri* to take the body of the Turkish Ambassador home from Washington very early in the Greek-Turkish crisis, when American policy was still ambivalent; or the Russians, in the earliest phase of the Berlin blockade, hinting that they were ready to hinder, reduce, or harass traffic into Berlin, but still with the bland official claim that the roads needed repair. Possibly, even, in the interwar period, Stalin's speech of 10 March 1939 dismissing the allegations of German designs on the Ukraine as a put-up job by the Western press, and saying that the Soviet Union would not be drawn into conflict to pull other people's chestnuts out of the fire for them. Probably the level of skill of the participants in a system of crisis management could be judged on their ability to resolve the ambivalences of this embryonic stage of policy in their own favour—or in the interests of peace. But sometimes it seems almost the case that a straw in the wind has *determined*, not merely *indicated*, which way the wind blows.

6

PROBLEMS AND PROSPECTS

ASSUMING that we are likely in the seventies to continue moving into a sphere of more conscious crisis management by the dominant powers, and that this is likely to change progressively from a two-power to a three-power enterprise, there are a number of questions we might ask about such a period. An obvious one is the question of how long it is likely to last. To this there are many possible answers, ranging from the dedicated pessimism which assumes that so complicated a system must produce a nuclear Armageddon by miscalculation within a very few years, to the determined optimism which assumes that men will forget their conflicts when the consequential dangers are demonstrated, and live in an unprecedented peace. My own answer would be tepidly optimistic: the society of states has succeeded in the past in managing its diplomatic conflicts so that any resultant hostilities stayed within some framework of prudence and restraint, and it may do so again. With a little luck, the secrets of the nineteenth century may be rediscovered at any moment. It is true that during the longest period of this sort, the Concert of Europe, there existed some specially favourable circumstances but the same may be said of the present. The favourable factors are quite different, but they are not the less favourable.

This answer does not depend on the assumption that the balance of forces will remain permanently triangular. On the contrary, it may well move towards a four-power and then a five-power concert, as Japan and some kind of European confederation move up the power scale. And these developments may not be more than fifteen years or so away. If it proves the case that the three-power balance is moving towards a five-power concert by the late 1980s, the parallels with some phases of the nineteenth century balance may become even more pronounced. Unfortunately, however, the most dangerous sector in this line of evolution may be the early years of the fully evolved triangular balance, probably the late 1970s. This period will carry a heavy load of uncertainties in the way of possible new weapons systems and certain new decision-makers, as well as representing the early and thus presumably costly part of the learning curve of crisis as a three-power game.

Before considering these prospects of the foreseeable future, it may be as well to look at some objections to the whole concept of crisis management. The first of these objections is moral. Crisis management is undoubtedly concerned with coercion: it involves, in Schelling's words, ' the manipulation of shared risk '. One of its analysts would define it simply as ' coercive diplomacy '. I would myself reject this definition as too narrow, since to my mind the study involves consideration of how and when to yield, as well as how and when not to. But no one could deny that the study of coercion, of allies as well as adversaries, is one strand in the study of crisis management. And Western liberals tend to assume, rightly, that coercion is rather a morally repellent enterprise, even when people are being coerced away from things they should not do anyway.

Someone once remarked that there are no clean hands in politics. This is even more true of international politics than of the domestic variety. The only plea one can put forward in mitigation is that, while crisis management does undoubtedly depend a good deal on communicated threat, it may still represent, in a given situation, the least of a number of evils. The management of the 1962 Cuban crisis is a good instance of this. The threat of an ultimate nuclear exchange was undoubtedly an element in this crisis, and it proved effective. Many people have said that even though it was effective, it was nevertheless deplorable that such a threat should have been used. Agreeing to deplore it, one may still hold that its consequences were less mischievous than the probable consequences of the alternative courses of action. The threat did not actually kill anyone, whereas the alternatives most debated in ' Excom ', invasion or airstrike, would undoubtedly have killed both Cubans and Americans. There was yet another possible choice: acquiescence in the Russian success, letting the Soviet technicians complete the installation of the missiles in Cuba. This would have been the most potentially disastrous result of all, not only because it would have encouraged and rewarded the streak of adventurism in Mr Khrushchev's policy, but because it would have raised the tension between Russia and America to such a level that war—perhaps central nuclear war—would almost certainly have eventuated between the two in the succeeding few years.

Schelling has put the basic point admirably:

What is in dispute is usually not just the momentary right of way, but everyone's expectations about how a participant will behave in the future. To yield is a signal that one can be expected to yield. To yield often or continuously may communicate an acknowledge-ment that that is one's role. To yield readily up to some limit, and then say ' enough ', may guarantee that the first show of obduracy loses the game for both sides.[1]

The last sentence is a neat encapsulation of what was wrong with the Western crisis management of the 1930s.

If one is looking for guidelines for the *threat* of force in crisis management one might well start with those for the *use* of force in the traditional theory of the just war, as elaborated by St Augustine and St Thomas Aquinas. Firstly for a just cause, secondly with a right intention, thirdly with a reasonable chance of success; fourthly if successful, it must offer a better situation than would prevail in the absence of action; fifthly force used (or threatened) should be proportional to the objec-tive sought (or the evil repressed). And sixthly it must be used with the intention of sparing non-combatants, and a reasonable prospect of doing so. These criteria seem as relevant in the nuclear age as they were in the fourth century. Incidentally, they would have ruled out the Vietnam war, which fails to meet the third, fourth, fifth and sixth requirements, and is doubtful on the first and second as well.

A second objection would be that crisis management on the nineteenth century model will not be practicable for present Western decision-makers because they are liable to be blown off the necessary diplomatic courses by a gale of dissenting opinion at home. To my mind this is not necessarily true, though the influence of dissenting opinion in various crisis-management episodes is a subject worth examining in more detail than is possible here. In almost every one of the crises looked at, it has been possible to hear an area, or several areas, of dissenting opinion: people who made demands for a course

[1] In a lecture quoted by Herman Kahn in *On Escalation* (1965), p. 225.

of action different from that chosen by the decision-makers. And these areas of dissenting opinion show themselves at every level below the chief decision-maker. Policy advisers near the chief decision-maker, such as high Foreign Office people in the Suez crisis, or the Chiefs of Staff in the Cuba crisis, articulate opinion like Opposition leaders, government backbenchers, editors and commentators, student demonstrators, polls: all these, it may be argued, have shown in various crises some ability to bring damaging pressure to bear on policy-makers, even if only to penalize them after the event by electoral means. The influence of dissident opinion has varied enormously from crisis to crisis in the selection looked at. It has been almost nil in crises little understood or regarded: the MLF, Skybolt, Laos, the Congo, Cyprus. Nor was it great in the Cuban missiles crisis, which developed so secretly and so swiftly that only the policy-makers knew what decisions had been made until it was too late to reverse them. On the other hand, British dissenting opinion had a considerable impact on the Suez crisis, in which it had the four months from July to October to gather force. And on Vietnam (which will be discussed in more detail presently) it has been the growth of American domestic resentment at a war which a large minority considered (in my view rightly) neither just nor in the national interest which has been the largest single factor in forcing the hand of successive Administrations in a way which must undoubtedly be considered detrimental to the objectives for which the war was (wrongly) undertaken.

The sharpest impact of dissenting opinion on crisis management in the interwar period was the blast of disapproval from British articulate opinion which greeted and killed the Hoare-Laval Pact, the scheme cooked up by Britain and France to save some of the territory of Ethiopia for the Emperor, and at the same time prevent the alienation of Italy from the Stresa front, with which they hoped to restrain Hitler in Europe. The Pact admittedly was in the worst tradition of European agreed depredations in the non-European world, and quite probably it might not have worked. Nevertheless its forced abandonment in the storm of moral indignation aroused when it was leaked prematurely (possibly by Laval) did nothing to save Ethiopia, which fell wholly into Italian hands four months later. And Mussolini, who had been prepared to move troops to the Brenner to block any gains by Hitler in the crisis over the murder of Dollfuss in 1934, was moved by the pressure of League efforts over Ethiopia to tie Italy to Germany's chariot wheels in the Pact of Steel. It would be difficult to show that the virtuous denunciation of the Hoare-Laval proposals, and their collapse, did anything either for the Ethiopians, or for peace, or for international morality, unless one believes in moral gestures for the sake of moral gestures.[2]

Among the postwar crises in which the influence of the opinion factor has to be considered, perhaps the most interesting is the Bay of Pigs crisis, the invasion of Cuba by US-sponsored Cuban refugee forces in 1961. This was probably the only crisis in which the critics of US policy had the chance—and had to face the responsibility—of perhaps making their will effective. There existed in American journalistic circles enough information on the training programme of the Cuban exiles and the intended invasion to raise the possibility of actually preventing the venture, if the papers printed all they knew or surmised. But this would have meant their being prepared to accept the danger of damaging the national interest, or the worse danger of crippling the project without preventing it, and so increasing the casualties among the invaders. In the event, the *New York Times* printed a report covering a good deal that was going on, but not all the information it had. At the time the editor got a sharp rebuke from President Kennedy. But a year later the President had changed his mind enough to say to the publisher that he wished the paper had printed *all* it knew. That is, he had by then become conscious that the pressure exerted on policy-formation by articulate dissident opinion might sometimes be valuable rather than mischievous.[3]

The reaction of decision-makers is not usually so philosophical.

[2] See F. S. Northedge, *The Troubled Giant* (1966), pp. 420 ff. for a fuller account of this crisis. Professor Martin Wight has pointed out that this episode was, nevertheless, probably the closest that the state system ever came, before or since, to applying sanctions against a great power.

[3] Various accounts of this episode have been given by those with personal knowledge of it. I have leant on reports of an account given by the Managing Editor of the *New York Times*, Mr Clifton Daniel, to the World Press Institute.

A long-drawn-out endurance of the pressures of criticism on some temperaments tends rather to create a sort of collective paranoia among those responsible for policy, in which any suggestion of alternatives seems a form of persecution, even betrayal. The attitude of President Johnson and those round him to the critics of the Vietnam war had by 1968 acquired this sort of quality, as witness his reaction to the Robert Kennedy 'peace feeler' of early 1968.

The most serious case against dissident opinion, however, is not its ambivalence in effect, or the wear and tear it creates in the nervous systems of policy-makers. It is that it may confuse the signalling system to the adversary by showing, so to speak, an apparent green light when the real lights are at red. If the adversary decision-makers come to overestimate the degree of influence of dissident opinion (if, for instance, Russian decision-makers had overestimated the influence of the American liberal-left in the first Berlin crisis) then the dissenters would be doing a grave disservice to crisis management. In fact on the record there is not much reason to doubt that the Russians have a good understanding of the relative weight to give to different sets of signals from the West. But the same may not be true of the Chinese. One might argue also that in the final crisis of the interwar period, Danzig 1939, Hitler may have been somewhat misled by some of the signals from non-official participants in the crisis management.[4]

The coming of the television 'global village' has of course greatly increased the moral tensions between the policy-makers and the electorate as far as acquiescence in actual military operations is concerned. Chamberlain, perhaps characteristically, foresaw this. He remarked in 1938:

Indeed, if it were not that China is so far away and the scenes which are taking place there are so remote from our everyday consciousness, I think the sentiments of pity, horror and indignation which would be aroused by a full appreciation of those events might drive this people to courses which perhaps they have never yet contemplated.[5]

---

[4] I am thinking of Dahlerus in particular; see A. J. P. Taylor, *The Origins of the Second World War*, pp. 271 ff.

[5] In the House of Commons, 21 June 1938, HC Deb., vol. 337, col. 936.

He was then speaking of the Japanese bombing in China. Vietnam is as far away as China, but full observation is now possible, by courtesy of the television news, and domestic revulsion against a remote war has certainly never before in history been as politically effective as it has been in America over the Vietnam war. Similarly in the Nigerian crisis, though it was possible to construct an intellectual case for backing the Lagos government against a proposed tribalist secession which might have been copied elsewhere in Africa, and have created greater disruption and misery, this intellectual case had a hard battle to stand up to the emotional impact of seeing the refugees of a Biafran village on television. The limit of Western moral acquiescence in certain kinds of military operations, especially long-drawn-out ones, is more uncertain than ever before. This is in general an excellent thing, and one must hope that a similar sensitivity will spread to the rest of the world. But it may well mean that Western participation in counter-insurgency operations must in future be ruled out as unfeasible for domestic political reasons, unless the moral case is absolutely watertight, which it seldom is in international politics.

If a process of joint crisis management outside their own respective bailiwicks develops between America and Russia, it will bring with it all the moral problems and incongruities of the ' imposed settlement '. Small powers involved with local adversaries are by no means likely to agree that settlements which seem reasonable to the dominant powers will also represent justice to themselves. The most flagrant interwar example of disregard of even the appearance of justice for a small power was, of course, the exclusion of Czechoslovakia from the Munich conference. It may be argued that in the longer run the Czechs did not really suffer as much by what was done to them in 1938 as they would have done if they, rather than the Poles, had provided the first battlefields of the Second World War. But this is not an argument which can be expected to appeal to small peoples when they see their interests bartered between the dominant powers. The West New Guinea (or West Irian) settlement is a good postwar example of how tangled the relation may be between justice and expediency in such cases. No one could pretend that the ' act of free choice' of 1969, which was the final outcome of a piece of crisis management by Robert Kennedy in 1962, and was attended by the panoply of 'UN supervision', represented actual self-determination for the Irianese. And self-determination is usually taken as the standard of international justice in these matters. Yet to promote the independence of the Irianese, a Stone-age people, and expect them to maintain it in the teeth of Indonesian resentment and their own economic weakness, might have been a still greater injustice to them than what was actually done.

It is impossible to leave this discussion of morality and expediency in crisis management without considering the case of Vietnam, though the problems it raises are so complex that one hesitates to treat them in as summary a fashion as is necessary here. One point which must be emphasized is that the original crisis mismanaged into war in Vietnam was that of 1946: an intramural crisis of the French sphere of power in Indo-China, which the French decided to 'resolve' by the use of military force. That first disastrous decision is in a sense the symbol of the entire abominable involvement, because what has been happening ever since is successive decisions by Western policy makers (first the French and then the Americans) that the military situation must be improved before a political settlement was possible. The final French disaster, Dien Bien Phu, was precipitated by precisely the same resolve. After 1954, one has to decide whether Vietnam ought to be considered one country with two claimant governments, respectively based in Hanoi and Saigon, and with areas of control divided by a temporary truce line at the 17th parallel pending political settlement, or as two countries, North and South Vietnam, divided by an international frontier. To my mind, every scrap of evidence points to the first interpretation, though some (not all) American international lawyers have argued for the second.[6] The

---

[6] The 1954 Geneva agreement specifically denies that the truce line at the 17th parallel could be considered a permanent frontier or partition: it was simply a truce line, north and south of which the respective armies would regroup, pending the political settlement through elections, originally scheduled for 1956. The two governments did not describe themselves as those of South and North Vietnam: they named themselves respectively the governments of the Republic of Vietnam and of the Democratic Republic of Vietnam. That is, *both* governments maintained

true character of American policy, if one makes this judgement, is that of great-power intervention in the civil war of a minor power. This intervention has passed through a number of phases: the supply of arms and money in the Eisenhower-Dulles period; the addition of advisers in the Kennedy period; the ' Americanization ' of the war with combat troops in the Johnson period; and then the ' Vietnamization ' of the war in the Nixon period. The basic political decision has, however, remained that taken in the Dulles period (the Pentagon papers apparently establish it as August 1954): the decision that a government friendly to the West must be maintained in South Vietnam because of the strategic importance of that area to the future of South-east Asia as a whole. This notion, encapsulated in the term ' domino-theory ', from the metaphor used by President Eisenhower in 1954 seems to have been based on a memory of how rapidly the Japanese overran South-east Asia in World War II, once they had moved into Vietnam.

The relevance of the parallel seems doubtful: the speed of Japanese advance owed a good deal more to their air and naval power, and to the absence of any efficient opposition in the rest of South-east Asia, than to the usefulness of bases in Vietnam. Moreover, the assumption that having Ho's writ run in South as well as North Vietnam represented an expansion of *China's* power-sphere revealed a total American incomprehension, at that time, of the relation of Hanoi to Peking. And in any case, even if excluding Ho from power in Saigon *was* strategically important to the West (which was always dubious) that would not morally justify turning South Vietnam into a battlefield.

Neither the moral nor the strategic case for the American intervention, therefore, seems convincing. But the point at issue for this study is the problem of great-power intervention in the civil wars of minor powers as one of the techniques of their management of the society of states. It must be conceded that this has been a regular and traditional technique in the field; if it had to be judged also a necessary or inevitable one, the whole concept of crisis management would seem unacceptable

that Vietnam was one country, and each of them claimed to be the legitimate government of that one country. The war between them therefore was a civil war, not an international war.

because of the potential moral costs both to the dominant power and the local power involved. But, on the evidence, it is not inevitable; indeed, its results this century have been so little rewarding to the dominant powers concerned that even on the most cynical basis of self-interest, the obvious principle is to avoid it at all costs.

Vietnam may well stand for centuries as the classic case of damage to the dominant power through such intervention, when one thinks of the ' fringe costs ' to the US: the alienation of a large sector of articulate young people from all the values of the American system, the worsening of the racial tensions at home, the inflationary spiral in the economy, the loss of self-confidence in the American élite. But even interventions which have been less costly, and appeared to have secured their immediate political objectives, have not necessarily ' paid-off ' diplomatically to the interveners. The intervention of Germany and Italy in the Spanish civil war secured the victory of the side they backed, but when Hitler and Mussolini tried to collect on the debts of gratitude due them from General Franco, they got singularly little for their pains. Hitler reflected that he would rather ' have three or four teeth taken out '[7] than enter negotiations with Franco again. The American intervention in the Chinese civil war (1945–8) had even more bitter and dysfunctional outcomes than the Western intervention in the Russian civil war. The British campaign in Malaya, 1948–60, might be considered an exception, if one is prepared to elevate the Emergency to the status of a civil war between the Chinese and Malay inhabitants of Malaya, though this would be rather a misreading of its character. But even stretching our category unduly to include this case, one could still say that the long-term diplomatic pay-off to Britain of the survival of the traditional political élite in Malaysia has not precisely been overwhelming.[8]

---

[7] *Ciano's Diplomatic Papers*, ed. Malcolm Muggeridge (London, 1948), p. 402.

[8] I have not included Korea in this list because the Western military operation there had much more the character of support to one party in an international war than intervention in a civil war. The distinction I am making, I would stress, is political and military, not legal. For some reason the doctrines of North Korea have not been able to evoke the kind of response in South Korea that the doctrines of North Vietnam have been able to evoke in South Vietnam. This may have

There is a sense in which Talleyrand's *mot* that non-intervention is a political and metaphysical term meaning much the same as intervention must always be the simple truth, as far as the dominant powers are concerned. That is, their policies are so important a factor in the fates of smaller powers that whatever they do influences the fortunes of the two sides in any civil or international war. In the Nigerian civil war, for instance, the British supply of arms to the Federal government was undoubtedly an intervention against Biafra. On the other hand, to cut off the supply of arms as some of the government's critics in Britain would have wished, would have been an intervention in favour of Biafra. But though the dominant powers can in this sense never entirely avoid intervening, they can make some choice about the degree of their intervention; and the direct use of the dominant power's own combat troops in large numbers, as with the Americans in Vietnam, represents a level of intervention that is almost always likely to portend disaster. The Chinese have a proverb that if you save someone from drowning, you are under an obligation to support him for the rest of his days. The Americans have saved a number of regimes in Asia from drowning, and the moral obligations for continued support that they have thus incurred had reached by Mr Nixon's time an almost intolerable level for the US electorate. Yet the process of America disembarrassing itself of these ' support costs ' is likely to be prolific of crisis. The operation may in some ways prove as delicate as removing the bottom layer from a house of cards.

To revert to Vietnam, its great failure as an exercise in crisis management was that the decision-makers concerned did not keep sight of their own first principle: that political ends should maintain ascendancy over military means in crisis decision-making. Partly because the military encounter was already under way when the Americans came in, so to speak, there has always been an overriding tendency in Vietnam to subordinate

something to do with the fact that the charismatic leadership resided in the North in the Vietnamese case and in the South in the Korean case, or it may have more complex economic and social causes. But its military effect has been that the strategic problem in South Korea is only the conventional international one of safeguarding a frontier, whereas the problem in South Vietnam has been that of also conquering a stubborn, determined, home-based faction in a civil war.

longer-term political ends to immediate military necessities, or assumed necessities. One can see this quite clearly in the 1970 American invasion of Cambodia. The invasion was officially justified, by the spokesmen of the Pentagon, on the grounds of its military utility and logic: the destruction of stores and the supply route of the other side, setting back their plans strategically by a year or so. Possibly if one were thinking only of the military objectives, it would seem justified in these terms. But the whole military operation is simply a means to a political end, and in this case the military advantage secured (probably short-term) was gained at the cost of incurring extra political burdens. Those political burdens were the increase of political responsibility for sustaining the Cambodian government (an obligation previously avoided because of Sihanouk's neutrality) and the increased alienation of the war-resistance party in America from the President's policies. Similarly with the 1971 invasion of Laos: again the military advantages of disrupting supply lines are bought only at the heavy political cost of further undermining the 1962 settlement, such as it was.

The most sophisticated justifications of the remaining American presence in Vietnam are those which argue that even though Vietnam has been a disaster, it must not be conceded to be a defeat. The essential argument is that for America to acquiesce in even a local defeat will damage its credibility in the central conflicts with China and the Soviet Union, and thus encourage those powers to more risk-taking policies. The obvious corollary of this view is that America cannot cut its losses in Vietnam until the situation looks like, at worst, a temporarily stable stalemate. And that means that American troops cannot make their exit until the South Vietnamese government appears likely to be able to sustain itself by the military efforts of its own armed forces, at least for a year or two.

One must concede that even a limited local defeat, if undisguised, is a very unpalatable dish for any President to swallow and to share with the electorate. Indeed its consequences for the attitude of the electorate towards America's world role in general are impossible to predict.[9] But against these arguments

[9] The domestic political effects of an undisguised defeat must also be considered. One might put it as a riddle: if the American domestic outcome of the stalemate

must be set the counter-argument that an essential element in maintaining the credibility of the leader of any enterprise is for him both to be and appear prudent and well-judging in estimating how much of the total available resources should be allocated to particular theatres of operations. A general determined to avoid defeat on one particular (and disadvantageous) battlefield may achieve a tactical victory there at the cost of an overall strategic disaster. If you fight too long on the wrong battlefield you may be unable to fight at all on the right ones.

The Middle Eastern area of crisis and potential crisis is in several respects more dangerous than that in South-east Asia. It is strategically of more direct importance to the dominant powers, since an unchecked Russian ascendancy there would have more influence on the balance of forces in the world than an unchecked Chinese ascendancy in South-east Asia. Also the local decision-makers in Israel and the Arab states are relatively less amenable to control by the dominant powers. Things can get out of hand more easily and rapidly, as one sees by looking at the crisis which produced the 1967 war. In the early stages of this crisis the Soviet Union appeared to be successfully manipulating the local powers. In May 1967 Soviet diplomats seem to have told the Syrians and Egyptians that Israel was massing about twelve brigades on the Syrian frontier preparatory to an attack intended to bring down the government in Damascus. The Egyptians moved troops into the Sinai Desert to draw Israeli forces away from the Syrian border, but they also asked the UN Emergency Force to leave, and closed the Straits of Tiran. To President Nasser's chagrin, U Thant (inspired by some legalistic views of the rights of the host power) did more than the Egyptians had intended. They were thus obliged to send troops to Sharm el-Sheik, and so, as President Nasser said, ' fell into the trap which had been laid for us '.[10] The Israelis attacked, and the Russians were obliged to work very hard diplomatically to ensure that they themselves were not drawn into a confrontation with the United

in Korea included McCarthyism, what is the potential outcome of a worse-than-stalemate result in Vietnam? Defeat does not usually sweeten the national temper of any country. Many US commentators argue that it would not be a true defeat. Their case may be the more useful even if the less convincing one.

[10] Interview in *Le Monde*, 19 Feb. 1970.

States, and to save their Arab clients from the consequences of their own military ineptitude. The Soviet Ambassador in Cairo was removed from Cairo three months after the war: possibly he incurred some of the odium of the defeat.[11]

The Middle Eastern crisis of summer 1970 exemplified still more clearly than that of 1967 the tendency of the dominant powers to move towards joint crisis management, using in this case—as in the crises of 1948, 1956, and 1967—United Nations processes as a mode of convenient diplomacy. (The exceptional role of the UN in Middle Eastern crises as against those elsewhere suggests that precedent may be an important factor, though obviously there are several others, in determining whether or not the UN will be chosen.) In terms of the classifications I have been suggesting, this was a case in which a local adversary crisis, between Israel and Egypt, touched off an intramural crisis for the Arab world as well as a domestic crisis for Jordan. Of the three dominant powers, two, the United States and the Soviet Union, were interested in stabilization and the restriction of hostilities: they acted through and on their respective client governments. China was interested in the continuance of conflict (or at least preventing American-Soviet ' collusion ') but its only mode of influencing the situation was through some of the guerrilla groups, and it was relatively ineffective.

The tendency that I have pointed out in other crises, for the most local power to be the most intransigent, because it has most to lose, is well illustrated here, for instance in a reported statement from Dr George Habbash that the Palestinian guerrillas would maintain their claims even at the cost of World War III.[12] In fact, however, by the hijacking of the British and American aircraft the guerrillas overplayed their hand (even though successfully dramatizing their case) and they came out of the crisis as net losers in terms of real power.

The only one of the three dominant powers whose policies can as yet be traced in any detail was the United States.

[11] For a fuller account of this crisis, see Michael Howard and Robert Hunter, *Israel and the Arab World: the Crisis of 1967* (London, Inst. for Strategic Studies, Adelphi papers, no. 41, 1967).
[12] See *The Times*, 16 Sept. 1970.

President Nixon and his advisers seem to have entered on a conscious course of managing the crisis before mid-September 1970. There were meetings of the preliminary crisis-management team, the Washington Special Action Group, on and after 15 September: Professor Kissinger, the Chairman of the Joint Chiefs of Staff Admiral Moorer, the Director of the CIA, the Deputy Secretary of Defense, and members of the State Department. The President, with obvious, conscious deliberation, signalled the level of American determination to have a hand in the outcome: hints of a possible US military intervention through the movements of the aircraft carriers *Saratoga*, *Independence*, *John F. Kennedy*, and *Guam*; the moving of a group of C-130 transport planes from Europe to Turkey; and the placing of an airborne brigade on semi-alert in Germany. The Russians apparently responded with a note saying that they had no intention of intervening in Jordan and were trying to discourage the Syrians from doing so. When the Syrians nevertheless moved troops into Jordan, a sharp American note was sent to Moscow indicating the gravest consequences if the Syrian forces did not withdraw. The Russian chargé d'affaires in Washington became involved in negotiations with Professor Kissinger and the State Department; the Syrian forces began to withdraw on 23 September, though perhaps as much for military reasons as because of Russian pressure.

One may perhaps assume that the sudden American release at this time of material concerning Soviet submarine-servicing facilities in Cuba (a project which had been under surveillance in Washington for months) was a signal intended as a general reminder to Russian decision-makers of the fragility of the *détente*, and the number of things that depend upon it, such as the SALT negotiations and the prospects of East-West relations in Europe, which in turn influence the Russian situation *vis-à-vis* China.[13]

The Middle East is obviously seen by the Soviet Union as too important an area of potential strategic gain to stay out of. Yet it is also one in which Russian decision-makers can hardly afford to let Soviet interests depend wholly on Arab capacities.

---

[13] See *Peking Review*, 25 Sept. 1970, for a somewhat feverish account of the American manoeuvres.

If the Suez Canal is to be reopened (which will greatly advance Soviet strategic interests in the Indian Ocean and Far East) it can only safely be done in the context of a bargain with the United States and Israel. A package deal which would have some advantages for each of the states involved, even the Egyptians, could obviously be devised, but hardly without a good deal of multilateral bargaining. The process of striking such a bargain, especially if it is extended over a long time, will represent as important a stage in the evolution of conscious joint crisis management by the dominant powers as the Cuban crisis, and may set still more important precedents.

This is because it entails a much more conscious and deliberate act of choice on the part of the dominant powers than the Cuban crisis. On that occasion they found themselves on a collision course which was relatively unexpected to both: in the Middle East they have each to manoeuvre difficult-to-control local allies who are by no means convinced of their own benefit from a projected settlement. In a sense it is the Cyprus situation transferred from the intramural to the adversary sphere of crisis management. In both cases the local communities see their respective interests as irreconcilable (Turkish and Greek Cypriots or Arabs and Israelis). But again in both cases, the outside great powers have strategic interests which they see as overriding, and some means of making them prevail: in Cyprus by direct control, on Suez by arms control. The reopening of the Canal, if it could be done under joint Soviet-American guarantee (a re-negotiation of the Treaty of Constantinople?) ought to maximize Soviet interest in the stability of the area, as it once did British interest when Britain was the dominant power there. The strategic cost to the West of this kind of settlement would be a more rapid build-up of Soviet power and influence in the Indian Ocean, but the United States would not necessarily, on present indications, see this as an insuperable obstacle. There are moderate economic gains to the Western powers and India to offset the strategic gains to the USSR.

The death of President Nasser, just as the first stage of the crisis had been surmounted, originally appeared likely to damage the prospects of the dominant powers contriving a settlement, since there appeared no other Arab leader in immediate prospect who might induce the Arab world to agree with what was devised. In fact, at the time of writing, this original assumption had been shown to be misleading: the new Egyptian decision-maker, President Anwar Sadat, *representing Egypt rather than the Arab world as a whole* appeared for that reason more, rather than less, able than President Nasser to move towards a recognition of Israel as a durable reality in the area. Soviet pressure towards a settlement which would include the reopening and protection of the Canal was quite clear: Sadat launched his diplomatic initiative after talks with the Russians.[14]

It is by no means true that crises have no useful function. They may indeed be useful enough to be ' manufactured to government order '. Possibly the Damansky Island crisis of early 1969 was of this character. That is, the original straying across the border of a Russian or Chinese patrol may have been accidental, and the reaction from the other side spontaneous, but the decision to ' play up ' the incident was a matter of convenience for both sides. The Chinese faced an imminent Party Congress, and found useful an incident on which to hang denunciation of the ' new Tsars ' and those within China who allegedly were interested in following the same path. The Russians faced a conference of other Communist parties, and found useful an incident which dramatized what they wanted to say about the belligerence of the Chinese. So the crisis was generally convenient, except to those who died.

In a larger and less cynical sense, crisis is probably a necessary evil in the assessment of claims for change. The interwar period was much concerned with what was then called ' the problem of peaceful change ', a rather ingenuous description of the issue, since the threat of force was always latent, just under the skin of the peace. But such a demand cannot be morally and politically discounted merely because it is accompanied by a hint of threat. The society of states, like other

[14] At the time of writing, the possible shape of the settlement seemed to include reopening the Canal, Israeli withdrawal some distance into Sinai, and a token Egyptian force on the far bank. The dominant powers' pressure on their respective clients has been visibly towards an outcome which will forward their common interest (also that of most of the society of states) in enough stability in the area to keep the Canal usable. This does little to resolve the conflict between Israel and the Arabs; only time for the growth of acquiescence can do that, and only if the time is well used.

societies, undoubtedly requires a mechanism for change. The traditional one has been war. Since we must assume that this mechanism ought to be discarded or discouraged, and must also concede that mechanisms based on true consent under law or arbitration are for the time being unlikely to be effective in real clashes of will or interest, there are not many potential modes of settlement available. Crisis provides a situation in which political resolution and military capabilities are measured against each other, to dramatize an act of choice, without war necessarily eventuating. Properly managed, it may ultimately enable states to write the peace treaties without first fighting the wars.

To say this is not to discount its potentialities for miscalculation and disaster. One of the prevalent causes of miscalculation, in both adversary and intramural crises, has been too low an estimate of the willingness of the other party to take risks. This in turn seems to derive chiefly from an underestimate of the forces pushing the decision-makers concerned to take action, and an overestimate of the forces restraining them from such action. In the Cuban missile crisis, the Americans found it hard to believe that the Russians would be rash enough to intrude militarily into a long-established sphere of American influence.[15] The Russians for their part underestimated, until the crunch, Kennedy's willingness to face a nuclear confrontation. The Vienna meeting, far from improving understanding between the two sides, may perhaps have led Khrushchev to a serious underestimate of Kennedy. Similarly in the Suez crisis, the Americans did not think the British would be rash enough to persist in the decision to use force, when they had been so strongly warned against it. And the British for their part seem to have believed that the Americans would not be tough-minded enough to use the sanctions they commanded

---

[15] The policy-makers in the Pentagon found this idea so incredible that a crisis-game scenario based on such a supposition was rejected only a few months before the actual event occurred. The crisis game as a dry-run for policy-makers who may actually have to face some day the real decisions that they 'game through' has been much cultivated in Washington since 1962, and has some dangers. See the author's 'A Game of Jeopardy', *Survival*, Sept. 1970, also Sidney F. Giffin, *The Crisis Game* (New York, 1965) and Andrew Wilson, *The Bomb and the Computer* (London, 1968).

against their own allies, once the adventure had been launched.[16] There is inevitably an element of wishful thinking in estimates of the other party's reaction to a course of action that one wishes to take.

There also seems to be a tendency for diplomatic defeat in a crisis, whether adversary or intramural, to act as an incentive to improving one's arsenal, in a way which may give the arms race, whether central or local, an extra spurt. The Cuban crisis was followed by enhanced Russian concentration on building both its missile forces, and its conventional naval forces, the two elements in which it had been at a strategic and tactical disadvantage in 1962. The Suez crisis hastened evolution to the Sandys defensive position of 1957–8, with its enhanced attention to British nuclear weapons. The Quemoy-Matsu crisis of 1958 provided China with uncommonly good reasons for the decision to build an independent nuclear armoury under its own control. The local crises of the Middle East and South Asia normally have an aftermath of efforts by the Arabs and the Israelis, or the Indians and Pakistanis, to obtain ever more sophisticated arms from the dominant powers. This does of course provide those powers with an extra mode of crisis management: the threat of interdiction of supply of new arms, and, especially, spare parts and ammunition. The Russians appear so far reluctant to use this mode of control, and it is difficult for the West to use it unless the Russians do. But given time and the growth of a Russian conviction that it is usually China which reaps the fruits of instability, there could easily develop a joint technique in this field.

Something must be said of those two over-simplified prescriptions often put forward as the whole basis of crisis management: appeasement and ' brinkmanship '. It is to be hoped that by now there is enough political sophistication in the analysis of diplomatic processes for a general understanding of how inadequate either of these is (or in fact the two of them together are) as a guide to policy-making. Unfortunately each of them seems to have an irreducible appeal to some political temperaments: appeasement to the more masochistic and

---

[16] On this point see the memoirs of Mr Harold Macmillan, iv *Riding the Storm, 1956–1959* (London, 1971).

guiltridden segment of the liberal left, and brinkmanship to the more combatant and tenacious segment of the right, especially ex-Marxists. Thus in any given crisis we must expect cries of alarm both from nature's appeasers (when any indication of a sticking-point is made) and from nature's brinkmen (when any bargaining ploy or concession is offered). The Chamberlain years are the most obvious exemplification of the limits of appeasement as a technique, and the Dulles years of the limits of brinkmanship.

To say this is not of course to deny that either of the concepts may be useful, when applied with a judicious regard to overall power relationships. As Herman Kahn has said: ' The slogan " appeasement never pays " is clearly a misleading summary. There are many cases where accommodation and flexibility have not only prevented war, but have led to détente, entente and friendliness.'[17] The trouble with the Chamberlain policy was not the concept itself, but the fact that it was used *vis-à-vis* a decision-maker, Hitler, who was unappeasable short of the general hegemony of Europe, and who intended to use that hegemony to maintain in the German sphere of power political values that were entirely abominable.

As for brinkmanship, it undoubtedly has had its successes. Mr Dulles's famous remark that ' the ability to get to the brink without getting into the war is the necessary art ' is *part* of the truth about international politics, and one must concede that his handling of the Quemoy-Matsu crisis of 1958 seems, at this distance in time, to satisfy the criteria I have suggested for success. But the tough-minded legalistic suspicion which he brought to all bargaining situations greatly limited him as a policy-maker. Though he talked a good deal about situations of strength, he does not seem to have recognized one when he was in it, in 1953–5 while the Soviet leadership was readjusting itself after Stalin's death.

The oversimplifications represented by appeasement and brinkmanship are easy enough to reject. There are others that are more tempting. One might for instance be inclined towards a generalization that if one power can force on its adversary the choice between raising the possible exchange

[17] *On Escalation*, p. 224.

from the local level to the strategic nuclear level, or else backing down, the power bearing the burden of nuclear decision will back down. In the Cuban missile crisis this proposition worked to the advantage of the Americans. They had a decisive tactical edge in local conventional forces, at sea, and the Russians could have countered their ability to impose the blockade only by resort to nuclear exchange (which they were inhibited from doing by their decisive strategic inferiority) or by counter-moving elsewhere, for instance Berlin, and taking the risks attendant on that. The Americans understood this well enough: there was a grim little exchange in Washington in which someone asked Kennedy ' Where will we be if they move on Berlin? ' and he replied ' In World War III '. Yet in a sense one can say it was the known weakness of the tactical situation of the West in Berlin which inhibited the Russians here: since the West obviously had no other resort but the nuclear one, the Russians were obliged to allow for this fact in their contingency planning.

In the *Pueblo* case, the principle worked against the Americans, in that the only usable strike-power the Americans had nearby was nuclear-armed, and they were rightly not willing to consider its use in such a situation. (There were of course other influences on this outcome.) In the Quemoy-Matsu crisis of 1958, the principle worked, at one remove, against the Chinese in the sense that if they were to persist in their efforts to take the islands, in the face of the enormous concentration of fire-power embodied in the US 7th Fleet, it could only be if the Russians were willing at necessity to raise the level of exchange to the nuclear one, and they were not so willing.

One might be inclined to think of this as history saying ' what I tell you three times is true. ' But it cannot be taken to mean that the power with the most immediately usable local strength in conventional forces will necessarily win, because if that were true the game over Berlin would have been long ago lost by the West. In fact what determines the outcome is a subtle balance involving both capability and will on several levels. On the capability side, overall nuclear strength can off-set local conventional weakness (as over Berlin) or vice versa (as over the *Pueblo*) or the one can reinforce the other (as over

Cuba). On the side of will, it would seem that the power with most at stake is in some curious way strengthened by the adversary's consciousness of that fact. This worked in favour of the US on both Cuba and Berlin. Thus all we can in general say is that in each of these crises the ' winner ' has been the power which made the shrewdest and most imaginative assessment of the adversary's will in a particular situation.

A shadow of ambiguity over a situation may be as effective as real strength. Indeed the use of ambiguity in a way that is creative rather than merely confusing, as I argued earlier, may be one of the more valuable skills in the field. But what might be called a central ambiguity (as against a peripheral one) is likely to be disastrous, and there is a sort of built-in tendency to such an ambiguity in what might be called the manic-depressive cycle in Western political societies. One can see this cycle very clearly by contrasting the American mood at a high point—say early 1963—and a low point, say early 1968. Early in 1963, with the Cuba victory secured, Kennedy in the White House, and ' Camelot-on-the-Potomac ' at its peak flowering-period, many people in America and elsewhere in the West saw America as the most creative and hopeful society in history. Only five years later, in March 1968, with Kennedy dead and Johnson politically broken, the problems of American society seemed so overwhelming as to cast real doubt on its ability to stay involved with the external world, or to preserve itself as a social entity. Though America represents the most extreme case, probably all the Western powers have some tendency to swing between seeing any defeat as a cataclysm, and seeing any victory as a triumphant end of the conflict, rather than as the beginning of the next round. The Marxist and especially the Maoist views of the world (the latter based on guerrilla experience) are in many ways better adapted to the process of continuous struggle, though they also have the weaknesses of their strength. ' Protracted war ' is their weapon: it cannot be America's.

Would it matter if the American mood of withdrawal extended beyond Vietnam to other commitments, and produced a period something like the isolationism of the twenties and thirties? To my mind this would be a disastrous development, creating a situation that I would be inclined to call ' ambiguity overload '. Winston Churchill, writing of the crisis slide before the First World War, said ' The terrible Ifs accumulate '. That is, the ambiguities overwhelmed the system. Similarly, in the foreseeable future, the spectacle of the strongest *status quo* power impotent or withdrawn from the contest would create so many uncertainties everywhere that the management structure would break down under the weight of them. The foreign policy objectives of any power are not something fixed, given, settled: they are a function of the opportunities open to it. And the withdrawal of America would reopen so many opportunities to, for instance, Russia and China, that it would become impossible to predict what objectives would reappear in their foreign policies. Even given a Vietnam settlement, American retreat into introspection as a result of domestic problems is not altogether beyond possibility, though it would probably take a condition approaching civil war to force such a general withdrawal on American policy-makers.

Hopefully disregarding this possibility, one comes to another problem which may be expressed by the phrase: who will be *tertius gaudens*? That is to say, which of the three dominant powers will be most in a position to manoeuvre, or shift its weight, *vis-à-vis* the quarrel between the other two? It probably depends on which of the three conflicts is the sharpest at any particular time: between China and Russia, between China and America, or between America and Russia. To my mind the most peremptory dispute for the immediate future is likely to remain that between China and Russia, and therefore the position of *tertius gaudens* for the time being falls to America. Thus American diplomacy may be able to some extent to ' work both sides of the street '. There can be no case, short of some unexpected turn of Chinese policy, for the Americans to commit themselves in any wholehearted or conclusive way to Russian purposes against China. They can do more, both for Western diplomatic objectives and for the preservation of peace by adopting a reserved or balancing position. The Russians are potentially in a vulnerable and discomforting situation, with a formidable enemy on their Far Eastern frontier, as well as unrest in their Western buffer zone, the

Warsaw Pact countries. If the tensions of this two-front position grow more acute, their interest in a new European security organization might become great enough to induce them to bargain something for it, even a tolerance of some restored internal freedom among the Warsaw Pact powers. But any kind of ' package deal ' which seemed to offer the Russians a free hand in the East against concessions in the West would contain greater dangers than those it resolved: dangers to the central power balance, that is, and these must be of more moment to the dominant powers than local interests, even in Europe.

Comparing the three spheres of potential crisis between the dominant powers—America/Russia, America/China and Russia/China—one would be obliged to judge that the America/ Russia sphere has seen the most development of conventions of crisis management, and the Russia/China sphere possibly the least, though of course Westerners are not in a very good position to judge this. In the America/China sphere the 1965-6 period, just after the American input of combat forces into Vietnam, represented the most dangerous corner since 1958, but in this crisis, as in earlier ones, some measure of agreement seems to have been established through the Warsaw talks. Communication between the United States and China was never, in fact, after 1954, as completely broken as many people supposed, though it was difficult, inadequate, and subject to static.

By mid-1971, with Dr Kissinger's visit to China and the project for Mr Nixon's, the process of establishment of tacit understandings, already far advanced between America and Russia, appeared to be developing surprisingly fast between America and China. This probably owed as much to a change in Chinese policy as to the effect of the Vietnam trauma on American policy. During late 1970 and early 1971 Chinese decision-makers appeared to be returning to the calculations of conventional diplomacy after the ' insurgents' international ' of the Cultural Revolution period. One may see this most clearly in the Chinese choice of options in the 1971 crises over Ceylon and Bangla Desh. In both instances the decision-makers in Peking chose to support the established government: in Ceylon against a far-left insurgency, in Pakistan against a left-nationalist recessionist insurgency. However disappointing these choices may have been to those who assumed that People's China would find it a moral duty to support revolutionary causes, it was a perfectly logical product of the Chinese national interest as calculated in traditional power-political terms. There were many other indicators of the same preoccupation: for instance, the Chinese welcome to the British government's proposal to join the EEC. United Europe is seen as a potential power rival both to the Soviet Union and the United States: hence its strengthening is to be welcomed—even if it is the capitalist world's most successful innovation in the postwar period. Perhaps the reconciliation of Maoist orthodoxy with increasing consciousness that national interests may be secured more readily by diplomatic manoeuvre is now the central intellectual preoccupation of Chinese policy-makers.

This bears upon the special problem made apparent in something which Mr McNamara once said when discussing the possible reasons for an American ABM system: that the United States had to guard against what he called an ' irrational ' decision by Chinese policy-makers in a crisis. ' Irrational ' is a word usually taken to imply an inability to relate means to ends, and it would be a very condescending view of the Chinese which attributed such a quality to them. But there is a sense in which one can say that Chinese judgements about the relations between ends and means seemed during the Cultural Revolution so different from Western or Russian judgements about the same relationship, that they were not predictable, and therefore decision-makers in other systems tended to choose the most pessimistic interpretation of them.

This problem in calculation is no longer so acute. A central question for judgement by the decision-makers in a crisis situation is *what degree of defeat* the adversary power will take before moving from crisis management to major hostilities. To my mind all three will take considerable local defeats before making this decision in the nuclear age. But it must remain necessary not only that each should be able to send and read signals about the limits of defeat in particular issues, but that each should have in the eyes of the others an assessable and rational view of what is a limited, and what an unlimited, defeat. That is, the assumption of rational behaviour is a condition for the growth of the system of conventions: it can be established only by communication between the dominant powers.

The whole domain of crisis management is a sort of no man's land sown with uncharted minefields of such problems. And it must be repeated that even a high rate of success in the management of crises does not necessarily end the underlying conflicts. One can quite imagine, for instance, the underlying conflict over the Middle East proving as durable in twentieth-century diplomacy, and as prolific of crises, as the Eastern Question—of which it is the lineal descendant—in nineteenth-century diplomacy. But if the society of states can learn to manage the crises, it may learn to live with the conflicts, even perhaps finding in them a source of moral and political development. Evolving the conventions which sustain order (or at least reduce the most damaging forms of disorder) opens one way towards the possibility of justice.

SELECT BIBLIOGRAPHY

Acheson, Dean. ' Introduction ' to *The United States in world affairs, 1947–1948*. New York, Harper for Council on Foreign Relations, 1948.
—— *Present at the creation: my years in the State department*. London, Hamish Hamilton, 1970.
Bell, Coral. *Negotiation from strength: a study in the politics of power*. London, Chatto & Windus, 1962.
Bridge, F. R. 'The diplomatic relations between Great Britain and Austria-Hungary.' Unpublished Ph.D. thesis of the University of London, 1966.
Buchan, Alastair. *Crisis management: the new diplomacy*. Boulogne-sur-Seine, Atlantic Institute, 1966.
Carr, E. H. *The twenty years' crisis, 1919–1939: an introduction to the study of international relations*. London, Macmillan, 1939.
—— *International relations between the two world wars (1919–1939)*. London, Macmillan, 1947.
Drummond, Roscoe and Gaston Coblentz. *Duel at the brink*. London, Weidenfeld & Nicolson, 1961.
Feiling, Keith Grahame. *The life of Neville Chamberlain*. London, Macmillan, 1946.
Fitzgerald, C. P. *The Chinese view of their place in the world*. London, OUP for RIIA, 1964.
Fleming, D. F. *The cold war and its origins, 1917–1960*. London, Allen & Unwin, 1961. 2 vols.
Kahn, H. *On escalation: metaphors and scenarios*. London, Pall Mall Press, 1965.
Kaufmann, William W. *The McNamara strategy*. New York, Harper & Row, 1964.
Kecskemeti, Paul. *Strategic surrender: the politics of victory and defeat*. New York, Atheneum Press, 1964.
Kennan, George. *Memoirs, 1925–1950*. London, Hutchinson, 1968.
Kennedy, R. *Thirteen days: the Cuban missile crisis, October 1962*. London, Macmillan, 1969.
Langer, William. *Explorations in crisis: papers on international history*, edited by Carl E. and Elizabeth Schorske. Cambridge, Mass., Belknap Press of Harvard Univ. Press, 1969.
Lefever, Ernest Warren. *Uncertain mandate: politics of the U.N. Congo operation*. Baltimore, Johns Hopkins Press, 1967.
Lippmann, Walter. *The cold war: a study in U.S. foreign policy*. London, Hamish Hamilton, 1947.
Loewe, M. *Imperial China*. London, Allen & Unwin, 1966.
Lorenz, Konrad. *On aggression*. London, Methuen, 1966.
Luard, Evan, ed. *The cold war: a reappraisal*. London, Thames & Hudson, 1964.
Medlicott, W. N., ed. *From Metternich to Hitler*. London, Routledge & Kegan Paul, 1963.

Nixon, Richard Milhous. *Six crises*. London, Allen & Unwin, 1962.

Northedge, F. S. *The troubled giant*. London, Bell, 1966.

Stephens, Robert. *Cyprus: a place of arms*. London, Pall Mall Press, 1966.

Taylor, A. J. P. *The origins of the second world war*. London, Hamish Hamilton, 1961.

Thomas, Hugh. *The Suez affair*. Harmondsworth, Penguin Books, 1970.

Wood, David. *Conflict in the twentieth century*. London, Institute for Strategic Studies, 1968. (Adelphi papers, no. 48.)

Young, Oran. *The intermediaries: third parties in international crises*. Princeton, NJ, Princeton UP, 1967.

—— *The politics of force: bargaining during international crises*. Princeton, NJ, Princeton UP, 1968.

Zanegin, B. N. *The nationalist background of China's foreign policy*. Moscow, Novosti Press Agency, 1968.

INDEX